The Dedollarization Paradigm

Rethinking Global Financial Systems

JARREL E.

Library of Congress Control Number: 2023921328

First edition

ISBN: 9798868935657

Contents

Dedication

This book is dedicated to the visionaries and trailblazers who dare to challenge the status quo and envision a more equitable and resilient global financial landscape. To those who understand that the evolution of our economic systems requires bold thinking, relentless inquiry, and a commitment to fostering positive change.

In the spirit of dedollarization, this dedication extends to the individuals, policymakers, scholars, and global citizens who contribute to the ongoing dialogue about the future of our interconnected world. May your endeavors inspire a paradigm shift that transcends borders, fosters cooperation, and shapes a financial system that truly serves the needs of diverse nations and their people.

Your unwavering dedication to rethinking global financial systems is a testament to the power of collective action and the pursuit of a more inclusive and sustainable economic future. May this work contribute to the discourse you have so boldly advanced, and may the ideas within these pages fuel further innovation and transformative initiatives.

Forward

In the dynamic landscape of global finance, the quest for a more resilient and equitable international monetary system has become imperative. "Dedollarization Paradigm: Rethinking Global Financial Systems" emerges as a pioneering exploration into the intricate web of economic dynamics, geopolitical shifts, and the evolving role of currencies in shaping the future of our interconnected world.

Authored by Jarrel E., this comprehensive volume navigates through the complexities of dedollarization—a phenomenon poised to redefine the traditional contours of the global financial architecture. As we embark on this intellectual journey, it is crucial to acknowledge the timeliness and relevance of the subject matter in a world where economic interdependence and geopolitical realignments underscore the need for a paradigm shift.

The dedollarization Paradigm is not merely an academic inquiry; it is a call to action, a reflection of the transformative forces that nations and financial institutions are grappling with. Through meticulous research, Jarrel unveils the historical roots, current challenges, and future possibilities inherent in the process of dedollarization. The narrative extends beyond the analysis of economic policies, encompassing the broader implications for political landscapes, social structures, and the very fabric of global governance.

Preface

One of the distinctive features of this work is its exploration of the multifaceted strategies employed by nations such as China and Russia in navigating the dedollarization terrain. Their roles as catalysts for change, as explored by Jarrel E., underscore the geopolitical dynamics at play and the potential ramifications for the future of global economic leadership.

As the book unfolds, it delves into the economic theories that underpin dedollarization and contemplates the practical implications for nations striving to extricate themselves from the pervasive influence of the US dollar. Digital currencies, bilateral agreements, and the reshaping of international financial institutions emerge as key components in the blueprint for a dedollarized future.

"Dedollarization Paradigm" transcends the boundaries of traditional economic discourse. It is a discourse on resilience, adaptability, and the imperative for nations to seize the opportunities embedded in this transformative shift. Jarrel presents not only a critique of the existing monetary system but a visionary roadmap for a more inclusive, diverse, and cooperative global financial architecture.

In the pages that follow, readers will encounter a wealth of insights, meticulously researched and eloquently presented. "Dedollarization Paradigm" invites policymakers, economists, scholars, and global citizens to engage in a dialogue that extends beyond the confines of academia—a dialogue that shapes the way we perceive, navigate, and ultimately transform the global financial systems of tomorrow.

As we embark on this intellectual odyssey, let the "Dedollarization Paradigm" serve as a guiding beacon—a source of inspiration, contemplation, and a catalyst for transformative action in the pursuit of a more equitable and resilient global financial order.

Introduction

In a rapidly evolving global landscape, the concept of dedollarization has emerged as a pivotal force reshaping the foundations of international finance and trade. The once unquestioned dominance of the U.S. dollar as the world's reserve currency is being challenged by a confluence of economic, geopolitical, and technological factors. This book embarks on a comprehensive exploration of this phenomenon, delving deep into the dynamics of dedollarization and its far-reaching implications for the global financial system.

As an author with a commitment to producing professional works, I understand the need for a meticulous examination of this transformative process. The pages that follow will unravel the historical context, drivers, and consequences of dedollarization, providing a nuanced understanding of the factors that are redefining the architecture of international finance.

The journey begins with a historical perspective, tracing the ascendancy of the U.S. dollar in global finance and revisiting the seminal moments in its history. The Bretton Woods Agreement, the petrodollar system, and the dollar's reign as the world's primary reserve currency are examined in detail, setting the stage for the subsequent analysis.

We will then explore the multifaceted forces propelling dedollarization. Economic considerations, the rise of alternative reserve currencies, and growing concerns over sovereign debt and currency risk will be dissected. Case studies of nations and regions actively pursuing dedollarization strategies, such as China, Russia, and the European Union, will provide real-world insights into this paradigm shift.

This book will not shy away from the complexities and challenges associated with dedollarization. We will address the implications for global trade, financial market stability, and the geopolitical realignments that are in motion. Moreover, the role of cryptocurrencies, particularly Bitcoin and the advent of Central Bank Digital Currencies (CBDCs), in this context will be thoroughly examined.

Challenges and risks inherent to dedollarization will be analyzed, along with policy recommendations designed to navigate the transition to a post-dollar world. Multilateral cooperation, financial system resilience, and strategies for currency diversification will be explored as potential paths forward.

The conclusion will serve as a synthesis of the key findings, emphasizing the ongoing evolution of global financial systems and the imperative for a new financial order. The future scenarios and predictions section will provide readers with a glimpse into what may lie ahead on the road to a multipolar financial system.

Throughout this book, you will find rigorously researched data, expert analysis, and a commitment to professionalism. The appendices will include essential statistical information, a glossary of terms for clarity, and a comprehensive reference section.

In an era where financial systems are undergoing a profound transformation, "The Dedollarization Paradigm" is your guide to understanding the forces at play and the potential outcomes. Join us in this intellectual journey as we reevaluate the very foundations of global finance and explore the possibilities of a post-dollar world.

Understanding the Dollar Dominance

let's explore the intricacies of understanding the dominance of the US dollar in the global economic landscape, drawing insights from historical foundations, economic advantages, geopolitical influence, challenges, and potential future scenarios.

- **Historical Foundations of Dollar Dominance:** The roots of the US dollar's dominance can be traced back to the Bretton Woods agreement of 1944, where it was established as the world's primary reserve currency, backed by the convertibility of gold. This historical foundation solidified the dollar's position and set the stage for its global prominence in trade and finance.
- **Reserve Currency Status and Economic Advantages:** The US dollar's status as the world's primary reserve currency

is a key pillar of its dominance. It comprises a substantial portion of global foreign exchange reserves, providing the United States with economic advantages such as lower borrowing costs and increased liquidity in global financial markets.

- **Trade Settlement and Financial Markets Infrastructure:** The widespread use of the US dollar in international trade simplifies transactions and fosters convenience. Moreover, the robust infrastructure of US financial markets, including the New York Stock Exchange and the US Treasury market, contributes to the dollar's attractiveness, serving as a cornerstone of global financial stability.

- **Geopolitical Influence and Soft Power:** Dollar dominance is intricately linked to the geopolitical influence of the United States. The use of the dollar in international transactions extends the reach of US economic policies and facilitates diplomatic leverage, highlighting the role of soft power in maintaining the dollar's supremacy.

- **The Federal Reserve and Global Monetary Policy:** The role of the US Federal Reserve in shaping global monetary policy adds another layer to dollar dominance. Central banks worldwide closely monitor and respond to Federal Reserve decisions, reinforcing the centrality of the US dollar in the international monetary system.

- **Challenges to Dollar Dominance:** While the dollar has long held its dominant position, challenges have emerged. The rise of alternative reserve currencies, coupled with efforts by some nations to dedollarize, poses potential threats to the traditional dominance of the US dollar in the global financial landscape.

- **Rise of Alternative Currencies and Geopolitical Shifts:** The emergence of alternative reserve currencies, such as the euro and the Chinese yuan, signals a shift in the global economic order. Geopolitical dynamics, including changing alliances and the rise of new economic powers, may contribute to a reevaluation of the relative strength of the US dollar.

- **Digital Currency Landscape and Central Bank Digital Currencies (CBDCs):** The advent of digital currencies, including the exploration of central bank digital currencies (CBDCs), introduces new complexities. CBDCs may influence the global currency hierarchy, challenging traditional systems and potentially reshaping the dynamics of international finance.

- **Global Economic Rebalancing and Collaborative Initiatives:** Ongoing efforts by nations to rebalance the global economic order present both challenges and opportunities. Collaborative initiatives, such as the development of regional currencies and economic alliances, could play a pivotal role in reshaping the narrative of dollar dominance.

- **Future Scenarios and Adaptation:** As the global economic landscape evolves, the future of dollar dominance remains uncertain. Adaptation to technological innovations, changing geopolitical dynamics, and collaborative efforts among nations will likely play a crucial role in shaping the trajectory of the US dollar's dominance in the years to come.

References:

- Eichengreen, B. (2011). Exorbitant Privilege: The Rise and Fall of the Dollar and the Future of the International Monetary System. Oxford University Press.

- Cohen, B. J. (2008). The Future of Money. Princeton University Press.
- Chinn, M. D., & Frankel, J. A. (2007). Will the Euro Eventually Surpass the Dollar as Leading International Reserve Currency? In G7 Current Account Imbalances: Sustainability and Adjustment (pp. 285-322). University of Chicago Press.
- Rey, H. (2015). Dilemma not Trilemma: The Global Financial Cycle and Monetary Policy Independence. Proceedings - Economic Policy Symposium - Jackson Hole, 285-333.

The Need for Dedollarization

The imperative for dedollarization arises from a confluence of economic, geopolitical, and financial considerations, prompting nations to reassess their reliance on the US dollar in global transactions. The historical dominance of the dollar, stemming from post-World War II agreements like Bretton Woods, has led to a concentration of economic power and influence in the hands of the United States. This concentration has created vulnerabilities for other nations, exposing them to the whims of US monetary policy and economic fluctuations.

Geopolitically, the need for dedollarization is underscored by a desire among nations to assert their economic sovereignty and reduce dependence on a single currency controlled by a singular global power. Political tensions and disagreements with the United States have prompted countries to seek alternatives, fostering the exploration of diversified currency reserves and avenues for economic autonomy.

Economically, the call for dedollarization is driven by a recognition of the risks associated with a sole reliance on the US dollar. Currency fluctuations and economic shocks linked to the dollar can have profound implications for the stability of national economies. Diversifying currency reserves becomes a strategic imperative to insulate nations from the potential negative impacts of a volatile dollar.

The development of regional currency blocs is one avenue through which dedollarization is pursued. Collaborative efforts among nations to establish or strengthen regional currencies provide a framework for reducing dependence on the dollar and fostering regional economic stability. This approach aligns with the broader goal of creating a more balanced and diversified global financial system.

The promotion of digital currencies, particularly central bank digital currencies (CBDCs), emerges as another facet of the dedollarization narrative. Digital currencies offer a technological means to facilitate cross-border transactions with reduced reliance on traditional fiat currencies. The exploration and implementation of CBDCs provide an innovative pathway for nations to navigate the dedollarization process.

Challenges associated with dedollarization include the need for careful currency risk management. Shifting away from the US dollar requires robust strategies to handle potential risks associated with new reserve currencies. Financial institutions play a crucial role in adapting to these changes, requiring them to reassess and adjust their services to accommodate a more diversified and dynamic monetary landscape.

Implications for global trade are significant in the dedollarization paradigm. As nations diversify their reserves and adopt alternative currencies, the dynamics of international trade relationships undergo transformation. This shift necessitates a reevaluation of trade policies, agreements, and the overall structure of global economic interactions.

The implementation of dedollarization strategies necessitates international collaboration and coordination. Institutions like the International Monetary Fund (IMF) play a pivotal role in facilitating dialogue and cooperation among nations as they navigate the challenges and opportunities presented by the dedollarization paradigm.

Policymakers are tasked with the responsibility of creating clear frameworks that promote stability during the transition to a dedollarized world. Transparent guidelines for currency transitions and monetary policies are essential to mitigate potential disruptions and ensure a smooth evolution of the global financial system.

In conclusion, the need for dedollarization emerges as a multifaceted imperative driven by geopolitical, economic, and financial considerations. As nations seek to diversify their reserves, establish regional currencies, and explore digital alternatives, the global financial landscape undergoes a transformation that requires careful management, collaboration, and adaptation by governments, financial institutions, and international organizations.

Scope and Objectives of the Book

The dedollarization paradigm explored in this book encompasses a vast and complex terrain within the realm of international finance and economics. The scope extends beyond a mere examination of surface-level phenomena, reaching deep into the intricacies of the global monetary system. By tracing the historical, economic, and geopolitical underpinnings of dedollarization, the book aims to present readers with a comprehensive understanding of the forces shaping this transformative shift.

The primary objective of this book is to unravel the multifaceted motivations and consequences associated with dedollarization. It seeks to demystify the process, providing readers with a nuanced perspective on the challenges and opportunities inherent in reducing reliance on the US dollar. Through a thorough exploration of case studies, economic theories, and geopolitical analyses, the book aims to equip readers with the knowledge necessary to navigate this evolving paradigm.

Furthermore, the book aspires to contribute to informed decision-making and policy formulation. By delineating the implications of dedollarization for nations, financial institutions, and the global economy, it seeks to offer insights that can guide stakeholders in adapting to and harnessing the potential benefits of this transformative shift. The objectives extend beyond presenting a mere chronicle of events; they encompass the facilitation of critical thinking and strategic planning in the face of evolving global economic dynamics.

In its exploration of the dedollarization paradigm, the book is not merely an observer; it is a catalyst for intellectual engagement. It aims to inspire curiosity, encourage thoughtful analysis, and foster a deeper understanding of the intricate web of factors influencing the trajectory of global finance. By addressing the broader implications of dedollarization, the book seeks to contribute to a more informed and participatory discourse on the future of the international monetary system.

The History of the US Dollar

The history of the US dollar in the global economy is a narrative intertwined with the evolution of modern finance. Born out of the aftermath of World War II, the Bretton Woods agreement in 1944 laid the foundation for the dollar's ascent to global dominance. Under this accord, the US dollar became the linchpin of the international monetary system, pegged to gold and serving as the primary reserve currency.

As the post-war era unfolded, the dollar's influence expanded exponentially. The Marshall Plan and the subsequent reconstruction efforts solidified the United States as an economic powerhouse, reinforcing the appeal of the dollar as a stable and reliable currency. This period marked the beginning of the dollar's journey as the cornerstone of global trade and finance.

The 1970s ushered in a transformative chapter with the collapse of the Bretton Woods system. President Richard Nixon's decision to abandon the gold standard severed the direct link between the dollar and gold, paving the way for a fiat currency system. This shift, while causing short-term turbulence, ultimately liberated the dollar from the constraints of gold convertibility and allowed for greater flexibility in monetary policy.

The 1980s witnessed the dollar's resilience as a safe-haven currency during times of global economic uncertainty. Its role as a haven for investors seeking stability became pronounced, contributing to the sustained global demand for the dollar. The rise of financial globalization further solidified the dollar's position, as it became the preferred currency for international trade and investment.

The turn of the millennium saw the euro emerge as a potential rival to the dollar. The creation of the Eurozone and the adoption of the euro as a common currency among member nations posed a challenge to the dollar's hegemony. However, the dollar maintained its dominance, buoyed by the enduring strength of the US economy and financial markets.

The 2008 financial crisis marked a pivotal moment in the dollar's history. While the crisis originated in the United States, the dollar paradoxically strengthened as investors sought refuge in its stability. This reinforced the perception of the dollar as a global safe haven, even in times of domestic economic turmoil.

In recent years, geopolitical dynamics have played a significant role in shaping the dollar's trajectory. US sanctions and trade policies have amplified discussions around dedollarization, with some nations exploring alternatives to reduce their dependence on the dollar. This has led to increased attention on digital currencies and the potential impact on the dollar's future role in the global economy.

The COVID-19 pandemic added another layer to the dollar's narrative. The unprecedented economic challenges prompted expansive monetary policies from the Federal Reserve, influencing global financial markets. The dollar's response to the crisis underscored its continued centrality in times of global economic upheaval.

As we navigate the complexities of the present, the history of the US dollar in the global economy serves as a roadmap for understanding its enduring significance. The dollar's evolution from the post-war era to the present day reflects a dynamic interplay of economic forces, geopolitical shifts, and financial innovations that continue to shape the trajectory of the international monetary system.

The Bretton Woods System and Dollar Hegemony

The Bretton Woods System, established in 1944, marked a pivotal moment in the history of global finance. Convened in the aftermath of World War II, the conference aimed to design a framework that could foster economic stability and prevent the currency-related challenges that contributed to the Great Depression. At the heart of this system was the commitment to peg currencies to the US dollar, which, in turn, was tied to gold. This decision granted the dollar a central role as the linchpin of the international monetary system, laying the foundation for what would become known as dollar hegemony.

Dollar hegemony, within the context of the Bretton Woods System, refers to the unparalleled influence and dominance of the US dollar in international trade and finance. The system established the dollar as the primary reserve currency, with other nations holding significant portions of their foreign exchange reserves in dollars. This bestowed upon the United States a unique privilege—the ability to finance its deficits by merely printing more dollars, as these dollars were in constant demand globally.

As the post-war era unfolded, dollar hegemony became increasingly evident. The Marshall Plan, designed to aid the reconstruction of war-torn Europe, facilitated the circulation of dollars abroad, solidifying the currency's role as a symbol of economic strength and stability. The willingness of other nations to hold dollars as a reserve asset further entrenched the dollar's hegemonic status.

The stability offered by the Bretton Woods System faced challenges in the 1960s, as the United States grappled with economic pressures, including rising inflation and trade deficits. By 1971, these challenges led then-President Richard Nixon to make the historic decision to abandon the gold standard, severing the direct link between the dollar and gold. This move, while ending the Bretton Woods System, did not diminish the dollar's dominance. On the contrary, it ushered in an era of fiat currency and allowed the dollar to float freely, further solidifying its hegemonic role.

Dollar hegemony's enduring legacy is observable in contemporary international finance. The dollar remains the world's primary reserve currency, facilitating global trade and investment. Many commodities, including oil, are priced and traded in dollars, reinforcing its status as the de facto global currency. The economic policies of the United States, particularly decisions made by the Federal Reserve, resonate globally, underscoring the far-reaching impact of dollar hegemony on the international monetary system.

Despite periodic challenges and discussions surrounding the potential shift away from dollar dominance, the resilience of dollar hegemony persists. The interconnectedness of global financial markets, the ubiquity of the dollar in international transactions, and the sheer scale of dollar-denominated assets contribute to the enduring influence of the US dollar in shaping the contours of the world economy. The Bretton Woods System may be a historical chapter, but its legacy in the form of dollar hegemony continues to shape the dynamics of global finance.

Dollar as the World's Reserve Currency

The designation of the US dollar as the world's reserve currency is a testament to its enduring significance in global finance. This status is not merely a consequence of economic strength but is deeply rooted in historical decisions and post-World War II financial arrangements.

The Bretton Woods System, established in 1944, played a pivotal role in solidifying the dollar's position as the world's primary reserve currency. Under this system, countries pegged their currencies to the US dollar, which, in turn, was tied to gold. The stability and economic prowess of the United States during this period made the dollar an attractive and reliable anchor for the international monetary system.

The collapse of the Bretton Woods System in 1971, marked by President Richard Nixon's decision to abandon the gold standard, did not diminish the dollar's role. Instead, it ushered in an era of fiat currency, where the dollar continued to be the linchpin of global finance. Nations around the world continued to hold significant portions of their foreign exchange reserves in dollars, a testament to the enduring trust and confidence in the currency.

The status of the dollar as the world's reserve currency is further underscored by its prevalence in international trade. Many commodities, including oil, are priced and traded in dollars, leading to a consistent demand for the currency. This dynamic creates a perpetual cycle where nations accumulate dollar reserves to facilitate trade, reinforcing the dollar's dominance.

The US dollar's role as the world's reserve currency is intricately tied to the unparalleled influence of the United States in shaping global economic policies. Decisions made by the Federal Reserve have far-reaching implications beyond US borders, affecting interest rates and monetary conditions worldwide. This interconnectedness amplifies the impact of the dollar on the stability and functioning of the international monetary system.

Despite periodic discussions and calls for diversification away from the dollar, the challenges of breaking free from the established system are formidable. The sheer scale of dollar-denominated assets, the ubiquity of the dollar in international transactions, and the network effects of existing financial infrastructure contribute to the resilience of the US dollar's status.

The dollar's role as the world's reserve currency is a double-edged sword. While it affords the United States unique economic advantages, such as lower borrowing costs, it also comes with responsibilities. The Federal Reserve must navigate its monetary policy with a global perspective, considering the impact on other nations and the potential for currency fluctuations.

Impact of Dollar Dominance on Global Trade and Finance

The impact of dollar dominance on global trade and finance is profound and multifaceted, shaping the dynamics of international economic interactions in significant ways.

Dollar dominance facilitates global trade by serving as the primary reserve currency. Many international transactions, including the pricing of commodities like oil, are denominated in dollars. This ubiquity simplifies trade relationships and fosters a level of convenience for nations engaged in global commerce. The widespread use of the dollar as a medium of exchange minimizes transaction costs and streamlines cross-border trade, contributing to the efficiency of the global trading system.

However, the reliance on the dollar in global trade also creates vulnerabilities. Currency fluctuations and changes in the value of the dollar can impact the cost and terms of trade for nations, especially those whose currencies are pegged to the dollar.

This dependence on a single currency exposes nations to the monetary policies and economic conditions of the United States, potentially influencing their economic stability.

In global finance, dollar dominance extends beyond trade to the realm of international finance and investments. The dollar's role as the primary reserve currency makes it a preferred choice for central banks and global investors. Countries hold significant portions of their foreign exchange reserves in dollars, considering it a safe-haven asset. This demand for dollar-denominated assets contributes to the stability of global financial markets.

The issuance of US Treasury bonds as a benchmark for safe and stable investments further solidifies the dollar's position. The high demand for these bonds reinforces the dollar's role as a global financial anchor, with the United States enjoying the privilege of funding its deficits at relatively lower costs. This dynamic contributes to the resilience of the dollar as a preferred currency for global financial transactions.

Despite the advantages of dollar dominance, it also poses challenges to the stability of the international monetary system. The concentration of economic power in the United States allows it to pursue expansive monetary policies, impacting global interest rates and liquidity. The Federal Reserve's decisions can have ripple effects on financial markets worldwide, requiring other nations to navigate the consequences of US monetary policy.

Moreover, dollar dominance has been associated with economic imbalances, as countries accumulate large dollar reserves to maintain exchange rate stability. This accumulation can lead to global economic distortions and trade imbalances, with surplus countries holding significant amounts of dollar assets.

In recent years, discussions around dedollarization have gained traction. Some nations, seeking to reduce their dependence on the dollar, explore alternative reserve currencies or promote the use of their own currencies in international trade. The rise of digital currencies, including central bank digital currencies (CBDCs), introduces another dimension to the conversation, potentially reshaping the landscape of global finance.

Challenges and Risks of Dollar Dependency

Dollar dependency, while offering certain advantages, also introduces a set of challenges and risks that can have profound implications for nations and the stability of the global economic system.

One of the primary challenges of dollar dependency lies in the exposure to currency risk. Nations that rely heavily on the dollar for international trade and hold substantial dollar reserves are vulnerable to fluctuations in the value of the dollar. Sudden changes in the exchange rate can impact the cost and terms of trade, affecting a country's economic stability and competitiveness on the global stage.

The dominance of the dollar also poses challenges related to monetary policy autonomy. Nations, especially those with currencies pegged to the dollar or extensive dollar-denominated debt, may find their domestic monetary policy constrained by the decisions of the US Federal Reserve. Changes in US interest rates and monetary conditions can have cascading effects, influencing inflation rates, capital flows, and overall economic stability in other parts of the world.

Economic imbalances are another significant challenge associated with dollar dependency. Surplus nations often accumulate large amounts of dollar reserves to maintain stable exchange rates, contributing to global trade imbalances. This imbalance can lead to distortions in the allocation of resources and create tensions in international trade relationships.

The risk of a sudden and substantial depreciation of the dollar is a concern for nations heavily dependent on it. Such a scenario can have severe consequences for economies with significant dollar-denominated debt, potentially leading to financial crises and economic downturns. The 2008 global financial crisis highlighted the interconnectedness of financial markets and the rapid transmission of shocks across borders.

Dollar dependency also amplifies the impact of US economic cycles on the rest of the world. Downturns or recessions in the United States can have spillover effects, affecting global demand for goods and services. This interdependence underscores the challenges of achieving economic stability when a single currency plays such a central role in the international monetary system.

The concentration of power and influence in the United States, as the issuer of the world's primary reserve currency, raises geopolitical risks. The use of the dollar as a tool for economic sanctions or trade policies can create tensions and conflicts, influencing diplomatic relationships and global geopolitical dynamics.

Efforts to dedollarize, while a potential solution to some of these challenges, also come with risks. The process of diversifying reserves and promoting alternative currencies requires careful management to avoid disruption and volatility in financial markets. Additionally, the transition away from the dollar may face resistance from existing financial institutions and established systems.

In conclusion, the challenges and risks of dollar dependency encompass currency volatility, constraints on monetary policy, economic imbalances, financial vulnerabilities, and geopolitical tensions. Navigating these complexities requires strategic policy making, risk management, and, potentially, efforts to diversify reserves and promote alternative currencies in the pursuit of a more stable and resilient global economic system.

Vulnerabilities in a Dollar-Centric System

A dollar centric global economic system, while providing certain advantages, is not immune to vulnerabilities that can have far-reaching implications for nations and the stability of the international monetary system.

One key vulnerability lies in the potential for currency volatility. The dominance of the US dollar means that fluctuations in its value can have cascading effects on global trade and financial markets. The interconnectedness of the world economy amplifies the impact of currency volatility, exposing nations to the risk of sudden and significant changes in exchange rates.

Another vulnerability stems from the interconnected nature

of global financial markets. The widespread use of the dollar in international transactions means that developments in the United States, particularly in its financial markets, can swiftly transmit shocks across borders. Financial crises or economic downturns originating in the US can have a contagious effect, affecting economies that are intricately linked to the dollar.

The reliance on the dollar as the world's primary reserve currency also creates vulnerabilities related to economic imbalances. Countries accumulate substantial dollar reserves to stabilize their currencies and facilitate international trade. However, this accumulation can lead to trade and current account imbalances, distorting the allocation of resources and potentially creating tensions in global trade relationships.

The potential for a sudden and substantial depreciation of the dollar is another vulnerability in a dollar-centric system. Nations holding significant dollar-denominated assets or debts may face severe economic consequences if the value of the dollar declines rapidly. This risk is particularly relevant for countries with extensive dollar-denominated debt, as a depreciation can increase the real burden of debt.

The concentration of power in the United States, as the issuer of the world's primary reserve currency, introduces geopolitical vulnerabilities. The use of the dollar in economic sanctions or trade policies can become a tool for exerting influence, creating geopolitical tensions and potentially leading to conflicts. This dynamic highlights the delicate balance between economic and geopolitical considerations in a dollar-centric system.

Efforts to dedollarize, undertaken by some nations seeking to reduce their dependence on the dollar, pose challenges to the existing system. The process of diversifying reserves and promoting alternative currencies requires careful management to avoid disruptions and uncertainties in financial markets. Additionally, the potential emergence of new global reserve currencies may introduce additional complexities and uncertainties.

In conclusion, vulnerabilities in a dollar-centric system encompass currency volatility, interconnected financial markets, economic imbalances, the risk of currency depreciation, and geopolitical tensions. Recognizing and addressing these vulnerabilities is crucial for enhancing the resilience and stability of the international monetary system. As the world continues to navigate the complexities of a global economy centered around the US dollar, proactive measures and strategic considerations are essential to mitigate potential risks and challenges.

Currency Crises and Their Effects on Emerging Economies

Currency crises cast a profound shadow over emerging economies, creating a ripple effect that touches various facets of their economic landscape. Characterized by abrupt and substantial depreciation of the domestic currency, these crises instigate a chain of economic challenges with enduring implications.

One prominent repercussion is the surge in exchange rate volatility. The rapid devaluation of the domestic currency disrupts the stability necessary for businesses and investors to plan effectively. Importers and exporters grapple with heightened uncertainty, complicating trade relations and decision-making processes.

The fallout extends to inflationary pressures. The diminished value of the domestic currency contributes to an increase in the cost of imported goods and raw materials, fostering inflation. This, in turn, erodes the purchasing power of consumers and poses a formidable challenge to central banks striving to maintain stability in price levels.

Emerging economies, often burdened with substantial foreign-denominated debt, bear the brunt of increased debt servicing costs. As the domestic currency weakens, the expense of servicing this debt escalates, straining both government finances and corporate balance sheets. The potential outcome may involve debt defaults and a destabilized financial environment.

To defend their currencies, central banks may resort to interest rate hikes. While this strategy aims to attract foreign capital and restore exchange rate stability, it simultaneously inflicts adverse effects on domestic businesses and consumers. Elevated interest rates elevate borrowing costs, impeding investment and consumption.

Economic contractions frequently accompany currency crises. The interplay of exchange rate volatility, inflation, and financial instability diminishes confidence among consumers and investors. This decline in confidence translates into reduced spending, diminished investment, and an overarching economic downturn.

The challenges extend to the balance of payments. While a weakened domestic currency can enhance export competitiveness, it simultaneously raises the cost of servicing foreign debt. Balancing these external pressures becomes a delicate task, and imbalances may persist, perpetuating economic difficulties.

Social and political unrest often burgeon in the wake of economic hardships induced by currency crises. Soaring inflation, rising unemployment, and growing income inequality sow dissatisfaction among the populace. Governments grapple with heightened pressure to implement reforms or confront the specter of political instability.

A currency crisis tarnishes a nation's reputation in the eyes of international investors, triggering a withdrawal of foreign capital. Rebuilding investor confidence necessitates sustained efforts to address underlying economic issues and enact structural reforms. The process is intricate, requiring a delicate balance to restore stability and attract renewed international trust.

In response to a currency crisis, governments and central banks must deploy swift and effective policy measures. Strategies such as capital controls, fiscal austerity, and structural reforms become imperative. The success of these endeavors hinges on their appropriateness, timeliness, and the cooperation of diverse stakeholders.

Geopolitical Implications of Dollar Supremacy

Dollar supremacy, the unparalleled dominance of the US dollar in the global economic arena, holds far-reaching geopolitical implications that extend well beyond the realms of finance. This preeminence of the dollar significantly influences the dynamics of international relations, geopolitical power structures, and the strategic interests of nations.

At its core, dollar supremacy provides the United States with a potent tool for economic leverage. The strategic use of the dollar allows the US to wield influence over global financial systems, enabling the imposition of sanctions and trade policies that shape geopolitical outcomes. This economic leverage becomes a key instrument in advancing and safeguarding the strategic interests of the United States.

The centrality of the dollar in global financial transactions affords the United States a commanding position in shaping the international financial system. This control over the financial architecture allows the US to dictate the terms of international trade, influence the rules governing financial institutions, and project economic power on a global scale. Consequently, the dominance of the dollar becomes a pivotal element in defining and reinforcing the economic dimensions of geopolitical power.

Nations heavily reliant on the dollar for trade and reserves often find their sovereignty intricately linked to the stability and policies of the United States. The influence the US wields over the global financial system can lead to dependencies that may compromise the autonomy of sovereign states. Economic sanctions or restrictions on access to the dollar become instruments through which the United States exerts considerable influence over the economic decisions and policies of other nations.

Dollar supremacy becomes entangled with geopolitical conflicts and international disputes. The ability to control financial flows through the dollar provides the United States with a strategic advantage in geopolitical maneuvering. Conversely, nations seeking to reduce their dependence on the dollar may explore alternatives, leading to shifts in geopolitical alliances and economic partnerships that redefine global power structures.

The dominance of the dollar extends into the realm of diplomatic relations, a phenomenon often referred to as "dollar diplomacy." The economic influence wielded through the dollar becomes a soft power tool that underpins diplomatic initiatives. By leveraging economic strength, the United States can advance diplomatic and strategic objectives, creating a nexus between economic power and international relations.

The structural reliance on the dollar within international institutions, including the International Monetary Fund (IMF) and the World Bank, reinforces the influence of the United States in these organizations. The dollar's role in transactions within these institutions contributes to shaping their policies and decisions, aligning them with the economic interests of the United States.

As nations explore alternatives and diversify their reserves away from the dollar, geopolitical dynamics may undergo significant shifts. The emergence of alternative reserve currencies or the utilization of regional currencies can challenge the traditional hegemony of the dollar, potentially leading to realignments in geopolitical influence and the distribution of global economic power.

The rise of digital currencies, especially central bank digital currencies (CBDCs), introduces a new and evolving dimension to the geopolitical implications of dollar supremacy. The development and adoption of digital currencies have the potential to reshape the landscape of global finance, with nations positioning themselves strategically in this emerging digital financial ecosystem.

In essence, dollar supremacy is not merely an economic phenomenon; it is a geopolitical force that intricately weaves economic power, international relations, and strategic interests. Understanding the geopolitical implications of the dollar's dominance is imperative for navigating the complex interplay between economics and geopolitics in the contemporary global landscape.

Case Studies of Successful Dedollarization

Examining case studies of successful dedollarization offers insights into the complexities and strategies involved in reducing dependence on the US dollar. These instances reveal nuanced approaches adopted by countries seeking to diversify their reserves and promote the use of alternative currencies in both domestic and international transactions.

One notable case is China's deliberate efforts to internationalize the renminbi (RMB). Recognizing the risks associated with a heavy reliance on the dollar, China has taken strategic steps to elevate the RMB's status. The establishment of offshore RMB markets, bilateral currency swaps, and the inclusion of the RMB in the International Monetary Fund's (IMF) Special Drawing Rights (SDR) basket have all contributed to the increased use of the RMB in global trade and finance. China's dedication to fostering the RMB as a viable alternative demonstrates a systematic and patient approach to dedollarization.

Another instructive case is that of Russia, which has actively pursued dedollarization as a response to geopolitical tensions. Russia's efforts involve reducing the share of US dollars in its reserves, diversifying into other currencies, and promoting the use of alternatives in international trade. The introduction of non-dollar trading mechanisms and agreements with several nations to conduct trade in local currencies showcase Russia's commitment to reducing reliance on the dollar in its economic interactions.

Venezuela provides a contrasting case, where external economic pressures and sanctions prompted a shift away from the dollar. Facing economic challenges exacerbated by US sanctions, Venezuela sought alternatives to the dollar for international transactions. This included exploring the use of its cryptocurrency, the Petro, and engaging in barter agreements with other nations to circumvent the constraints imposed by dollar-centric financial systems.

Furthermore, the European Union's experience with the euro offers insights into a successful regional dedollarization effort. The euro, introduced as the common currency for a significant bloc of nations, has become a viable alternative to the dollar in international trade and finance. The Eurozone's collective approach to promoting the euro as a reserve currency demonstrates the potential for regional cooperation in dedollarization endeavors.

These case studies highlight that successful dedollarization requires a multifaceted strategy. Key elements include the development of alternative currencies, the establishment of diverse trading mechanisms, and, in some cases, regional collaboration. The cases also underscore the importance of a long-term perspective and adaptability to navigate the challenges associated with reducing dependence on the US dollar. Successful dedollarization is often a gradual process, shaped by a combination of economic, geopolitical, and strategic considerations that vary across nations and regions.

Examples of Countries Transitioning from Dollar Dependency

Several countries have undertaken efforts to transition away from dollar dependency, reflecting a broader trend of dedollarization in the global economic landscape. These examples showcase diverse strategies and motivations behind reducing reliance on the US dollar.

China: China stands out as a prominent example of a country actively working to diminish its dollar dependency. In its pursuit of internationalizing the renminbi (RMB), China has established offshore RMB markets, engaged in bilateral currency swaps with various nations, and secured the inclusion of the RMB in the International Monetary Fund's (IMF) Special Drawing Rights (SDR) basket. These initiatives reflect a deliberate strategy to elevate the RMB's status, encouraging its use in global trade and finance and reducing dependence on the dollar.

Russia: Facing geopolitical tensions and economic sanctions, Russia has actively sought to reduce its reliance on the dollar. The country has taken steps to diversify its reserves by decreasing the share of US dollars, engaging in currency swaps with trading partners, and promoting the use of alternative currencies in international transactions. Russia's efforts exemplify a strategic approach to dedollarization driven by a desire to mitigate external vulnerabilities and enhance economic resilience.

Iran: In response to US-led sanctions, Iran has pursued dedollarization to protect its economy from the impact of restricted access to the dollar-dominated international financial system. Iran has sought to conduct trade in alternative currencies, entered into non-dollar agreements with trading partners, and explored the use of cryptocurrencies to facilitate transactions. These measures reflect an adaptive response to economic constraints imposed by dollar dependency.

Venezuela: Facing economic challenges and US sanctions, Venezuela has explored alternatives to the dollar. The country introduced its cryptocurrency, the Petro, as a means to bypass dollar-centric financial systems and facilitate international transactions. Additionally, Venezuela has engaged in barter agreements with other nations, emphasizing a shift away from traditional dollar-based trade. The Venezuelan experience underscores the motivation to find creative solutions when confronting external economic pressures.

European Union (Eurozone): The Eurozone provides a unique example of a regional effort to reduce dollar dependency. The introduction of the euro as a common currency for a significant bloc of European nations aimed to establish an alternative to the dollar. The euro has become a viable option for international trade and finance within the Eurozone, reflecting a collective approach to dedollarization through regional cooperation.

These examples illustrate the diverse strategies employed by countries to transition away from dollar dependency. Whether driven by geopolitical considerations, economic sanctions, or a desire to enhance monetary sovereignty, these efforts reflect a broader trend of dedollarization shaping the evolving dynamics of the global economic system. Successful transitions often involve a combination of developing alternative currencies, engaging in regional collaborations, and adapting to the changing landscape of international finance.

Lessons Learned from Their Experiences

The experiences of countries transitioning away from dollar dependency offer valuable lessons that can inform future dedollarization efforts. These lessons encompass strategic, economic, and geopolitical considerations, shedding light on the complexities and challenges associated with reducing reliance on the US dollar.

- **Strategic Diversification:** One crucial lesson is the importance of strategic diversification. Countries seeking to reduce dollar dependency should adopt a multifaceted approach that includes the development of alternative currencies, fostering regional collaborations, and exploring innovative financial instruments. Diversifying not only reserves but also trade and investment mechanisms can enhance resilience to external economic pressures.
- **Long-Term Perspective:** Dedollarization is a gradual process that requires a long-term perspective. China's deliberate efforts to internationalize the RMB and Russia's

strategic approach demonstrate the significance of patience and persistence. Rapid and abrupt transitions can introduce volatility and uncertainties, while a measured and sustained approach allows for a smoother adaptation to new economic realities.

- **Geopolitical Considerations:** Geopolitical considerations play a significant role in dedollarization efforts. Countries facing geopolitical tensions or economic sanctions, such as Russia and Iran, often prioritize reducing dependence on the dollar as a means of safeguarding their economic sovereignty. Understanding the geopolitical implications and crafting policies that align with national interests are critical aspects of successful dedollarization.
- **Adaptability and Innovation:** The experiences of Venezuela and Iran underscore the importance of adaptability and innovation in dedollarization efforts. These countries explored unconventional solutions, including the introduction of a national cryptocurrency (Petro) and the use of barter agreements, showcasing the need to be flexible and creative in responding to economic challenges and constraints.
- **Regional Collaboration:** The European Union's regional approach with the euro highlights the potential benefits of collaborative efforts. Regional collaboration can amplify the impact of dedollarization initiatives, providing collective strength and support. The Eurozone's success in establishing the euro as a viable alternative to the dollar underscores the advantages of regional integration in reducing dependence on a single currency.
- **Economic Resilience:** Dedollarization is often driven by the desire to enhance economic resilience. Countries that successfully reduce dollar dependency, like China and Rus-

sia, strengthen their ability to withstand external shocks and economic pressures. Building a resilient economic framework involves not only diversifying currency holdings but also implementing structural reforms and policies that foster stability.

- **Adapting to Digital Transformations:** The rise of digital currencies, as seen in Venezuela's use of the Petro, highlights the evolving nature of currency systems. Dedollarization efforts need to adapt to digital transformations in the financial landscape. Countries exploring digital currencies or engaging in technological innovations demonstrate an awareness of the changing dynamics of global finance.

Strategies for Implementing Dedollarization

Implementing dedollarization requires a comprehensive and strategic approach, encompassing various economic, financial, and policy measures. Countries seeking to reduce their reliance on the US dollar can consider the following strategies:

Develop Alternative Reserve Currencies: A fundamental strategy for dedollarization involves diversifying foreign exchange reserves by incorporating alternative currencies. This may include increasing holdings in currencies like the euro, Chinese renminbi (RMB), Japanese yen, or other stable currencies. Developing a diversified basket of reserve currencies helps mitigate risks associated with currency volatility.

Promote Regional Currency Arrangements: Encouraging the use of regional currency arrangements can enhance dedollarization efforts. Regional trade agreements and currency swap arrangements among neighboring countries facilitate transactions in local currencies, reducing dependence on the dollar. The European Union's success with the euro exemplifies the positive impact of regional currency collaboration.

Strengthen International Financial Institutions: Countries can work towards strengthening international financial institutions, such as the International Monetary Fund (IMF), to reduce the dominance of the dollar. This may involve advocating for reforms in the allocation of Special Drawing Rights (SDRs) to increase the role of alternative currencies in the global monetary system.

Facilitate the Use of Alternative Currencies in Trade: Encouraging the use of alternative currencies in international trade agreements is a practical strategy. Bilateral and multilateral trade agreements that allow transactions in currencies other than the dollar can contribute to dedollarization. This approach involves creating a supportive regulatory and financial infrastructure for diverse currency transactions.

Develop Local Currency Markets: Developing local currency markets can contribute to dedollarization at the domestic level. This includes fostering robust foreign exchange markets for local currencies, promoting the use of local currencies in trade transactions, and encouraging the issuance of local currency-denominated bonds.

Strengthen Financial Infrastructure: Enhancing domestic financial infrastructure is critical for successful dedollarization. This involves improving the efficiency and stability of financial systems, developing deep and liquid markets for alternative currencies, and ensuring that businesses and financial institutions have the necessary tools and mechanisms to transact in diverse currencies.

Encourage the Use of Digital Currencies: The rise of digital currencies, including central bank digital currencies (CBDCs), presents an opportunity for dedollarization. Countries can explore the development and adoption of digital currencies to facilitate cross-border transactions, reduce reliance on traditional banking systems, and promote financial inclusion.

Pursue Monetary Policy Independence: Countries aiming to dedollarize can pursue monetary policy independence. This involves adopting policies that prioritize domestic economic goals rather than being overly influenced by external factors, such as US monetary policy. A more independent monetary stance can contribute to reducing vulnerability to external economic shocks.

Diversify Foreign Investments: Diversifying foreign investments away from dollar-denominated assets is a key component of dedollarization. Countries can explore opportunities to invest in assets denominated in alternative currencies, such as foreign bonds and equities, to reduce exposure to fluctuations in the value of the dollar.

Develop Financial Education and Awareness Programs: Building awareness and understanding among businesses, individuals, and financial institutions about the benefits and risks of dedollarization is crucial. Financial education programs can help promote the use of alternative currencies, facilitate smoother transitions, and foster confidence in diverse currency transactions.

Currency Diversification and Its Role in Dedollarization

Currency diversification plays a pivotal role in the broader process of dedollarization, offering nations a strategic avenue to reduce dependence on the US dollar and enhance economic resilience. At its core, currency diversification involves the intentional allocation of foreign exchange reserves and trade transactions in a variety of currencies beyond the traditional reliance on the dollar. This strategy aims to mitigate the inherent risks associated with an exclusive focus on a single currency and fosters a more balanced and adaptable financial ecosystem.

One primary aspect of currency diversification in dedollarization efforts lies in the development and promotion of alternative reserve currencies. Nations actively seek to expand their holdings in currencies such as the euro, Chinese renminbi (RMB), Japanese yen, and others. This deliberate shift away from an overreliance on the dollar helps safeguard against the volatility and uncertainties associated with fluctuations in the value of a single currency, promoting stability in the management of foreign exchange reserves.

Moreover, in the context of international trade, currency diversification involves advocating for and facilitating transactions in currencies other than the dollar. Bilateral and multilateral trade agreements that permit the use of alternative currencies contribute to reducing the dollar's dominant role in global trade. This approach not only enhances economic sovereignty but also fosters a more inclusive and cooperative international economic environment, emphasizing the importance of a diverse array of currencies in global transactions.

Currency diversification also underscores the significance of regional collaboration in dedollarization efforts. Regional currency arrangements, such as currency swap agreements and collaborative trade pacts, promote the use of local currencies within a specific geographical area. This approach not only reduces dependency on the dollar but also strengthens regional economic integration, fostering greater financial stability and resilience to external economic shocks.

In conclusion, currency diversification emerges as a strategic imperative in the process of dedollarization. By intentionally expanding the array of currencies in foreign exchange reserves and trade transactions, nations can navigate the challenges associated with dollar dependency, mitigate economic vulnerabilities, and contribute to a more balanced and resilient global economic landscape. The pursuit of currency diversification represents a nuanced and strategic approach that aligns with the broader goals of economic stability, independence, and adaptability in an evolving international monetary system.

Benefits of Currency Diversification for National Economies

Currency diversification offers numerous benefits for national economies, providing a strategic approach to manage risks, enhance economic resilience, and promote financial stability. These advantages extend across various dimensions, contributing to a more robust and adaptable economic framework.

One of the primary benefits of currency diversification is risk mitigation. By holding a diversified portfolio of foreign currencies in their reserves, nations can reduce exposure to the volatility and uncertainties associated with a single currency, such as the US dollar. This risk mitigation strategy becomes particularly crucial during periods of currency fluctuations or economic downturns, providing a buffer against adverse external conditions.

Enhanced economic resilience is another significant advantage of currency diversification. Nations that diversify their currency holdings are better equipped to withstand external shocks, including fluctuations in exchange rates and global economic uncertainties. This resilience is particularly valuable in times of financial crises or disruptions, allowing countries to navigate challenges more effectively and maintain stability in their economic systems.

Promoting financial stability is a key outcome of currency diversification. By reducing reliance on a single currency, such as the US dollar, national economies can create a more balanced and stable financial environment. This stability extends to both domestic and international transactions, fostering confidence among businesses, investors, and consumers and minimizing the potential for abrupt economic disruptions.

Currency diversification also enhances monetary sovereignty for nations. By holding a diverse range of currencies in reserves, countries reduce their susceptibility to external economic pressures and mitigate the influence of monetary policies in the currency of a dominant nation. This increased sovereignty empowers nations to pursue independent monetary policies aligned with their specific economic needs and goals.

Moreover, currency diversification contributes to a more inclusive and cooperative global economic landscape. Encouraging the use of alternative currencies in international trade fosters collaboration and economic partnerships among nations. This diversity in currency transactions promotes a sense of economic equality and reduces the dominance of any single nation, fostering a more balanced and harmonious global economic system.

In the context of trade, currency diversification facilitates more flexible and efficient cross-border transactions. Bilateral and multilateral trade agreements that allow the use of diverse currencies simplify trade processes and reduce the reliance on a single medium of exchange. This streamlining of trade mechanisms contributes to smoother international commerce, benefiting both exporting and importing nations.

Evaluating Alternative Reserve Currencies

Evaluating alternative reserve currencies is a nuanced process that involves careful consideration of various economic, financial, and geopolitical factors. Nations seeking to diversify their foreign exchange reserves must assess the suitability and stability of potential alternatives, recognizing that the choice of reserve currencies has significant implications for the country's economic resilience and monetary sovereignty.

One critical aspect of evaluating alternative reserve currencies is the economic strength and stability of the currency in question. Nations often consider currencies issued by economically robust and well-managed countries, as these currencies are more likely to maintain stability and retain value over time. The strength of a currency is closely tied to the economic fundamentals of the issuing country, including factors such as GDP growth, inflation rates, and fiscal policies.

Geopolitical considerations also play a substantial role in the evaluation of alternative reserve currencies. Nations assess the political stability and global influence of the countries associated with the currencies under consideration. A currency issued by a politically stable and influential nation is generally perceived as a more secure store of value. Additionally, geopolitical alliances and collaborations can impact the willingness of nations to adopt a particular currency as part of their reserves.

Another crucial factor is the liquidity and depth of the currency's financial markets. A highly liquid currency facilitates smoother transactions and is more readily accepted in global trade. The existence of deep and well-functioning financial markets de-nominated in the alternative currency is essential for ensuring that nations can efficiently manage and trade their reserves.

The role of the currency in international trade is a key consideration in the evaluation process. Currencies widely used in global trade transactions offer greater versatility and acceptance, making them more attractive as reserve currencies. The ability of the currency to facilitate international trade and serve as a medium of exchange is essential for its viability as an alternative reserve currency.

Furthermore, the presence of a well-established and credible financial infrastructure is critical. Nations evaluating alternative reserve currencies seek assurance that the financial institutions supporting the currency are transparent, well-regulated, and capable of withstanding economic shocks. A robust financial infrastructure contributes to the stability and reliability of the alternative currency as a reserve asset.

The potential for currency appreciation or depreciation over time is a consideration that influences the evaluation process. Nations aim to hold reserves in currencies that are expected to maintain or appreciate in value, preserving the purchasing power of their holdings. Projections regarding future exchange rate movements and economic conditions contribute to the assessment of a currency's long-term viability as a reserve asset.

Challenges and Obstacles in Adopting Multiple Currencies

The adoption of multiple currencies in a national economy, while presenting potential benefits, is not without its share of challenges and obstacles. One significant challenge lies in the complexity of managing and regulating a multi-currency system. Coordinating the circulation and exchange rates of different currencies within a single economic framework requires a sophisticated regulatory infrastructure to ensure stability and prevent distortions in pricing and trade.

A key obstacle is the potential for increased transaction costs and logistical complications. Businesses and financial institutions may face challenges in managing multiple currencies, leading to added administrative burdens and increased costs associated with currency conversion. This can be particularly burdensome for small businesses and individuals engaged in cross-border transactions, potentially hindering economic activities.

Exchange rate volatility poses another challenge in a multi-currency environment. The values of different currencies can fluctuate based on various economic factors, introducing uncertainties for businesses and consumers. Such volatility may impact pricing strategies, trade balances, and overall economic planning, requiring nations to implement effective risk management mechanisms to mitigate the adverse effects of currency fluctuations.

The coexistence of multiple currencies can also lead to uneven economic development and regional disparities. Certain areas may experience currency appreciation, attracting investments and driving economic growth, while others may face depreciation and economic challenges. Balancing the economic impacts across different regions becomes a delicate task for policymakers, requiring targeted interventions to address disparities and promote inclusive development.

Inflation differentials among the adopted currencies represent a notable obstacle. If one currency experiences higher inflation than others, it can lead to distortions in pricing and purchasing power. Managing these inflation differentials requires vigilant monetary policies and coordination among central banks to ensure a harmonized economic environment.

Additionally, the potential for speculative activities and currency manipulation introduces risks in a multi-currency system. Traders and investors may exploit differences in exchange rates or engage in speculative activities, creating challenges for maintaining stable and well-functioning currency markets. Effective regulatory measures are crucial to curb such activities and uphold the integrity of the multi-currency system.

Political considerations add another layer of complexity. Differences in economic and monetary policies among countries contributing to the multi-currency system may lead to tensions and disagreements. Harmonizing policies and fostering cooperation becomes essential to prevent conflicts that could undermine the stability of the adopted currencies.

Finally, public awareness and education about the functioning of a multi-currency system are critical. Ensuring that businesses, financial institutions, and the general public understand the implications and mechanisms of using multiple currencies is vital for the successful adoption of such a system. Lack of awareness may result in confusion, resistance, or inefficient utilization of the available currencies.

The Role of Central Banks in Dedollarization

Central banks play a pivotal role in dedollarization initiatives, influencing and implementing policies that guide the transition away from excessive reliance on the US dollar. Their actions and decisions have far-reaching implications for a nation's monetary policy, economic stability, and the overall success of dedollarization efforts. Here are key aspects of the role of central banks in dedollarization:

Monetary Policy Formulation: Central banks are responsible for formulating and implementing monetary policies that directly impact a nation's currency composition. In the context of dedollarization, central banks may adopt policies that encourage the use of alternative currencies, such as promoting the issuance and circulation of domestic or regional currencies in trade and financial transactions.

Currency Reserves Management: Central banks manage a country's foreign exchange reserves, and the composition of these reserves is a crucial element in dedollarization. Central banks can actively diversify their reserves by increasing holdings in alternative currencies, reducing reliance on the US dollar. This strategic management of reserves contributes to economic resilience and reduces vulnerability to external shocks associated with dollar fluctuations.

Currency Swap Agreements: Central banks can engage in currency swap agreements with other central banks, facilitating trade and financial transactions in local currencies rather than the US dollar. These agreements promote the use of alternative currencies in cross-border trade, contributing to dedollarization efforts. Currency swaps also enhance financial cooperation between nations, fostering economic stability.

Promotion of Alternative Payment Systems: Central banks can encourage and support the development of alternative payment systems that facilitate transactions in currencies other than the US dollar. This may involve the establishment of regional payment platforms or the adoption of digital currencies, providing viable alternatives to traditional dollar-centric payment systems.

International Collaboration: Central banks often engage in international collaborations and negotiations that impact the global monetary system. In the context of dedollarization, central banks can collaborate with other nations to advocate for reforms in international financial institutions, including the International Monetary Fund (IMF), to reduce the dominance of the US dollar in the global financial architecture.

Development of Regional Currency Arrangements: Central banks may actively participate in the development of regional currency arrangements. Collaborative efforts to promote the use of regional currencies in trade and financial transactions contribute to dedollarization at a regional level. The European Union's adoption of the euro is an example of a successful regional currency arrangement.

Financial Stability Oversight: Central banks monitor and assess the overall financial stability of their economies. In the process of dedollarization, central banks need to carefully evaluate the potential risks and challenges associated with a shift away from the US dollar. This includes addressing issues such as exchange rate volatility, liquidity concerns, and the impact on the domestic financial system.

Communication and Public Awareness: Central banks play a crucial role in communicating dedollarization objectives to the public, financial institutions, and businesses. Public awareness campaigns and transparent communication regarding the benefits and risks associated with dedollarization efforts are essential to garner support and ensure a smooth transition.

Central Banks' Policies and Strategies for Reducing Dollar Dependency

Central banks implement a range of policies and strategies to reduce dollar dependency within their respective economies. One fundamental approach involves the active promotion of alternative currencies, often domestic or regional, to diversify the currency composition in trade and financial transactions. Central banks may incentivize businesses and individuals to utilize these alternative currencies, fostering a more balanced and resilient monetary ecosystem.

Monetary policy plays a pivotal role in central banks' efforts to diminish dollar dependency. By adjusting interest rates, managing liquidity, and influencing exchange rates, central banks can shape the attractiveness of alternative currencies. This approach aims to create a favorable environment for the adoption and use of non-dollar currencies, steering economic agents away from exclusive reliance on the US dollar.

Engaging in currency swap agreements represents another key strategy employed by central banks. These agreements enable transactions to be conducted in local currencies, reducing the need for the US dollar as an intermediary. By fostering bilateral or multilateral arrangements with other central banks, nations can facilitate trade and investment in alternative currencies, contributing to the broader objective of dedollarization.

Central banks may actively participate in the development and promotion of regional currency arrangements. These collaborative efforts involve the adoption of a common currency within a specific geographical region, as seen in the Eurozone with the euro. Regional currencies enhance economic coop-eration, streamline cross-border transactions, and reduce the dominance of the US dollar in intra-regional trade, exemplifying a strategic approach to reducing dollar dependency.

In addition to tangible currency initiatives, central banks play a crucial role in advocating for reforms in international financial institutions. By actively participating in global discussions and negotiations, central banks can contribute to reshaping the international monetary system, reducing the disproportionate influence of the US dollar. This diplomatic engagement aligns with the broader objective of fostering a more equitable and diverse global financial architecture.

To address the challenges associated with dedollarization, central banks often implement financial stability oversight measures. This involves a careful evaluation of potential risks and vulnerabilities arising from a reduced reliance on the US dollar, including exchange rate fluctuations and impacts on domestic financial systems. Central banks employ prudential regulations and risk management strategies to ensure a smooth and stable transition.

Furthermore, central banks may explore innovative payment systems and financial technologies to facilitate transactions in alternative currencies. Embracing digital currencies or supporting the development of efficient cross-border payment platforms contributes to the broader dedollarization agenda, providing practical solutions for businesses and consumers to transact in diverse currencies.

Communication and public awareness initiatives represent a critical aspect of central banks' policies for reducing dollar dependency. Transparent and effective communication helps garner support from the public, businesses, and financial institutions. Central banks articulate the benefits of dedollarization, address concerns, and ensure that stakeholders understand the rationale behind adopting a more diversified currency framework.

In summary, central banks deploy a multifaceted approach, encompassing monetary policies, currency swap agreements, regional collaborations, international advocacy, financial stability oversight, technological innovations, and communication strategies, to actively reduce dollar dependency within their economies. These concerted efforts reflect the central banks' role as architects of monetary policies that shape the trajectory of their nations' economic landscapes.

Strengthening Financial Stability in the Dedollarization Process

Strengthening financial stability is a paramount consideration in the dedollarization process, ensuring that the transition away from heavy reliance on the US dollar occurs smoothly and without causing disruptions to the domestic financial system. Central to this objective are several strategies and measures implemented to fortify financial stability during dedollarization:

Prudent Reserve Management: Central banks play a crucial role in managing foreign exchange reserves, and during dedollarization, a prudent approach involves diversifying these reserves. By holding a well-balanced mix of alternative currencies, central banks can mitigate the risks associated with currency fluctuations and enhance the overall stability of their reserves.

Robust Risk Management Frameworks: Incorporating robust risk management frameworks is essential to identify, assess, and mitigate potential risks arising from dedollarization. This includes evaluating the impact of exchange rate volatility, liquidity challenges, and the potential consequences on domestic financial institutions. Implementing effective risk management strategies helps cushion the financial system from potential shocks.

Regulatory Reforms and Oversight: Enhancing regulatory oversight is crucial to address the challenges that may emerge during dedollarization. Central banks may introduce regulatory reforms to adapt to the changing currency landscape, ensuring that financial institutions operate within a framework that supports a more diverse range of currencies. Clear and adaptive regulations contribute to the stability of the financial sector.

Collaboration with Financial Institutions: Central banks collaborate closely with financial institutions to navigate the dedollarization process. This involves providing guidance on risk management practices, facilitating the adoption of alternative currencies in financial transactions, and ensuring that institutions are well-prepared for the evolving monetary environment. Collaboration fosters a unified and coordinated approach to maintaining financial stability.

Development of Alternative Payment Systems: Investing in the development of alternative payment systems is instrumental in strengthening financial stability. The introduction of efficient and secure payment platforms that support transactions in various currencies reduces reliance on traditional dollar-centric systems. These alternative payment systems contribute to the seamless functioning of the financial ecosystem during dedollarization.

Public Awareness and Education: A well-informed public is a critical component of financial stability during dedollarization. Central banks engage in public awareness campaigns to educate businesses, individuals, and financial institutions about the benefits and implications of adopting alternative currencies. A knowledgeable public is better equipped to navigate the changing monetary landscape, reducing uncertainties and potential disruptions.

Stress Testing and Scenario Analysis: Conducting stress tests and scenario analyses is a proactive measure undertaken by central banks to assess the resilience of the financial system. These exercises help identify vulnerabilities and potential areas of concern, allowing central banks to implement preemptive measures and ensure that the financial system can withstand shocks associated with dedollarization.

International Cooperation: Given the interconnected nature of the global financial system, international cooperation is essential. Central banks collaborate with their counterparts in other nations to share best practices, coordinate policies, and address cross-border implications of dedollarization. This cooperation contributes to the overall stability of the international monetary system.

Collaborative Efforts Among Central Banks

Collaborative efforts among central banks are essential in fostering a cooperative and stable global financial environment. These collaborative initiatives aim to address shared challenges, promote economic resilience, and contribute to the overall effectiveness of monetary policies. Here are key aspects of collaborative efforts among central banks:

Information Sharing and Coordination: Central banks engage in the exchange of information and coordinate policies to enhance their collective understanding of global economic trends. Regular communication helps central banks stay informed about monetary policies, market developments, and potential risks, fostering a shared knowledge base that contributes to more effective decision-making.

Currency Swap Agreements: Central banks often enter into currency swap agreements with each other. These agreements facilitate the exchange of currencies between two central banks for a specified period. Currency swaps enhance liquidity in financial markets, provide a mechanism for managing short-term imbalances, and contribute to overall financial stability. These agreements strengthen the collaborative ties between central banks.

International Monetary Policy Coordination: Coordinated monetary policy actions among central banks are crucial, especially during times of global economic challenges. Collaborative efforts to align interest rate policies or implement synchronized interventions in currency markets aim to stabilize the international financial system and mitigate the impact of economic downturns.

Financial Stability Oversight: Central banks collaborate on maintaining and enhancing financial stability. This involves joint efforts in monitoring systemic risks, conducting stress tests, and developing policies to address vulnerabilities. Shared insights and coordinated oversight contribute to a more resilient global financial system, reducing the likelihood of widespread financial crises.

Development of Financial Standards: Central banks collaborate with international financial institutions to develop and implement financial standards. These standards, such as those established by the Basel Committee on Banking Supervision, contribute to the stability and soundness of financial institutions globally. Central banks' joint commitment to adhering to these standards fosters a harmonized and well-regulated financial environment.

Crisis Management and Contingency Planning: In times of financial crises, central banks collaborate on crisis management and contingency planning. Joint efforts may include coordinated interventions, liquidity support, and information sharing to address systemic challenges. Collaborative crisis management is crucial for stabilizing markets and preventing the contagion of financial instability.

Capacity Building and Technical Assistance: Central banks extend support to each other through capacity building and technical assistance programs. Collaborative efforts in training and knowledge transfer strengthen the capabilities of central banks, particularly those in developing economies. This fosters a more inclusive and cooperative global financial system.

Adherence to International Agreements: Central banks collaborate to uphold international agreements that govern financial and monetary interactions. Adherence to agreements such as those established by the International Monetary Fund (IMF) fosters trust and cooperation among central banks, contributing to the smooth functioning of the international monetary system.

Global Policy Coordination during Crises: In times of global economic crises, central banks engage in coordinated policy responses. Collaborative efforts may involve interest rate adjustments, liquidity injections, and other measures aimed at stabilizing financial markets and supporting economic recovery. Global policy coordination enhances the effectiveness of monetary policies and promotes a synchronized response to global challenges.

Impacts of Dedollarization on Trade and Investment

The process of dedollarization, or the reduction of reliance on the US dollar in international trade and investment, carries significant impacts on global economic dynamics. One notable effect is the potential shift in the landscape of international trade patterns. As countries diversify their currency usage, trade transactions may involve a broader range of currencies, fostering a more multipolar trading system. This can lead to increased currency risk management for businesses and necessitate adjustments in trade agreements to accommodate a more diverse currency environment.

Dedollarization also has implications for the stability and valuation of currencies involved in trade. As countries transition away from the US dollar, the value of alternative currencies may experience fluctuations. This can introduce uncertainties for businesses engaged in cross-border trade, requiring them to adapt to changes in exchange rates and potentially impacting the pricing of goods and services in international markets.

Moreover, dedollarization may influence global investment patterns. The US dollar has traditionally been a dominant currency for international investments and transactions. As the role of the dollar diminishes, there could be a reevaluation of investment portfolios and a shift towards assets denominated in alternative currencies. This could impact the allocation of capital across different regions and industries, prompting investors to consider a more diverse range of currencies in their investment strategies.

The effects of dedollarization on financial markets should also be considered. Changes in currency preferences may lead to adjustments in foreign exchange markets, impacting liquidity and introducing new dynamics to currency valuations. Investors and financial institutions may need to adapt their risk management strategies to navigate the evolving currency landscape, potentially affecting the overall stability of financial markets.

In terms of global economic governance, dedollarization may influence the role and functions of international financial institutions. The International Monetary Fund (IMF) and other global organizations may need to adapt to a more diverse set of reserve currencies, reflecting the evolving nature of the global economy. This could necessitate reforms in international financial structures to accommodate the changing dynamics of currency usage.

Additionally, dedollarization may have geopolitical implications. The US dollar's historical role as the world's primary reserve currency has been closely tied to American influence in global affairs. A reduction in the dollar's dominance could lead to a rebalancing of geopolitical power dynamics, with implications for international relations and economic alliances.

Rebalancing Trade Relations in a Dedollarized World

In a dedollarized world, the rebalancing of trade relations becomes a pivotal aspect of the evolving global economic landscape. As countries reduce their reliance on the US dollar in international trade, a fundamental shift occurs in the dynamics of trade partnerships and agreements. Rebalancing trade relations involves a recalibration of economic ties, with a focus on diversifying currency usage and fostering a more equitable distribution of trade benefits.

One significant aspect of rebalancing trade relations is the negotiation and establishment of trade agreements that accommodate a multipolar currency environment. Countries may seek to diversify the currencies used in bilateral and multilateral trade deals, reducing the dominance of any single currency. This necessitates a more inclusive approach to trade negotiations, where currencies beyond the traditional US dollar play a prominent role in facilitating transactions.

The rebalancing process also entails a reassessment of trade imbalances and the pursuit of fair and mutually beneficial trade practices. With the reduction of the US dollar's centrality, countries may explore mechanisms to address trade inequities and promote a more symmetrical flow of goods and services. This could involve discussions on tariff structures, non-tariff barriers, and trade facilitation measures to create a level playing field for nations using diverse currencies.

Moreover, the rebalancing of trade relations in a dedollarized world involves a strategic reevaluation of supply chains and production networks. Countries may seek to enhance regional economic integration, promoting trade within geographic proximity and fostering stronger economic ties. This regional focus allows nations to capitalize on complementary strengths, reducing dependence on global trade routes dominated by a single currency.

Currency risk management becomes a central consideration in the rebalancing process. Businesses engaged in international trade need to adapt to a more varied currency environment, requiring sophisticated risk mitigation strategies. Currency hedging, financial instruments, and collaborative efforts between governments and businesses are integral components of managing the complexities associated with currency diversification.

Additionally, the rebalancing of trade relations involves a commitment to transparent and open economic policies. Countries may engage in dialogue to establish common standards and practices that promote fair competition and market access. This collaborative approach fosters an environment where nations feel confident in the stability and predictability of their trading partners, contributing to the overall success of dedollarization efforts.

The transformation of trade relations in a dedollarized world extends beyond economic considerations to geopolitical dimensions. As nations diversify their trade alliances and partnerships, geopolitical alignments may shift, influencing global power dynamics. The rebalancing process presents opportunities for emerging economies to play more substantial roles in the global economic order, contributing to a more multipolar and interconnected world.

Attracting Foreign Investment in Dedollarized Economies

Attracting foreign investment in dedollarized economies represents a multifaceted challenge and opportunity. As nations reduce their reliance on the US dollar, creating an environment that encourages foreign investors to participate in the economic landscape becomes crucial. One key element in this effort is the establishment of transparent and investor-friendly policies. Dedollarized economies must articulate clear regulatory frameworks, ensuring that foreign investors can navigate the business landscape with confidence, understanding the rules and protections in place.

Another pivotal factor is the stability of the local currency. In a dedollarized context, demonstrating a commitment to maintaining a stable and well-managed currency is imperative. Central banks play a vital role in implementing sound monetary policies that foster confidence in the local currency. A stable currency environment reduces uncertainty for foreign investors, encouraging long-term commitments and facilitating the growth of foreign direct investment.

The diversification of investment options denominated in various currencies is essential for attracting foreign capital. Dedollarized economies should actively promote investment opportunities in sectors where transactions are conducted in alternative currencies. This involves creating mechanisms, such as investment instruments and financial platforms, that facilitate seamless transactions in diverse currencies, thereby broadening the appeal to a global investor base.

Collaborative efforts between governments and the private sector are crucial in promoting foreign investment. Governments can engage in targeted promotion and marketing campaigns to showcase the investment potential of their economies. Simultaneously, fostering partnerships with international financial institutions and industry associations enhances the visibility of dedollarized economies, instilling confidence in potential investors.

To attract foreign investment, dedollarized economies must focus on infrastructure development. Robust infrastructure, including transportation, energy, and communication networks, not only enhances the overall business environment but also signals a commitment to sustainable economic growth. Foreign investors are more likely to engage in economies with well-developed infrastructure, as it reduces operational costs and increases the efficiency of business operations.

Moreover, the implementation of investor-friendly legal frameworks and dispute resolution mechanisms is paramount. Dedollarized economies should ensure that legal systems are transparent, fair, and efficient. Establishing clear mechanisms for resolving disputes and protecting the rights of foreign investors contributes to a stable investment climate, fostering trust in the judicial processes.

Promoting technological advancements and innovation is another avenue for attracting foreign investment. Dedollarized economies that position themselves as hubs for technological development, research, and innovation can attract investments from industries seeking growth opportunities in a dynamic and forward-thinking environment. Governments can incentivize research and development activities, creating a conducive ecosystem for technological investments.

Promoting Financial Inclusion and Access to Global Markets

Promoting financial inclusion and access to global markets is a critical endeavor with profound implications for economic development and shared prosperity. The intersection of inclusive financial services and global market access creates opportunities for individuals, businesses, and nations to participate more equitably in the global economy. Here are key considerations in promoting financial inclusion and facilitating access to global markets:

Expanding Access to Banking Services: Financial inclusion begins with providing basic banking services to individuals who are traditionally excluded from the formal financial system. Initiatives such as the establishment of mobile banking, simplified account opening procedures, and community banking programs contribute to bringing unbanked or underbanked populations into the financial mainstream, laying the foundation for broader market participation.

Leveraging Financial Technology (FinTech): The integration of financial technology plays a pivotal role in promoting financial inclusion and facilitating access to global markets. Innovative solutions, such as mobile payment platforms, digital wallets, and online banking services, empower individuals who lack traditional banking infrastructure to engage in financial transactions. FinTech enhances efficiency, reduces costs, and broadens the scope of financial services globally.

Microfinance and Small Business Support: Promoting financial inclusion involves supporting microfinance institutions and facilitating access to credit for small and medium-sized enterprises (SMEs). Microfinance initiatives provide crucial financial services to entrepreneurs in underserved communities, fostering economic empowerment and entrepreneurship. Enabling small businesses to access global markets amplifies the impact of these initiatives, contributing to economic growth.

Financial Education and Literacy Programs: Educating individuals about financial principles and practices is fundamental to fostering financial inclusion. Financial education programs empower individuals to make informed decisions about saving, investing, and participating in global markets. Improved financial literacy enhances individuals' confidence and capability to engage with diverse financial products and services.

Building Inclusive Payment Systems: Modernizing payment systems to be inclusive and interoperable is essential. Inclusive payment systems facilitate domestic and international transactions, enabling individuals and businesses to seamlessly participate in global markets. Cross-border payment platforms that accommodate diverse currencies contribute to breaking down barriers and fostering global economic integration.

Regulatory Inclusivity and Consumer Protection: Creating regulatory environments that encourage innovation while ensuring consumer protection is vital. Balanced regulatory frameworks promote the development of diverse financial services, including those that facilitate global market access. Regulations that safeguard consumer rights and privacy build trust in financial systems, encouraging broader participation.

International Collaboration and Partnerships: Promoting financial inclusion requires collaborative efforts on a global scale. International organizations, governments, financial institutions, and technology providers can form partnerships to share best practices, develop inclusive financial infrastructure, and address challenges collectively. Collaborative initiatives contribute to creating a more connected and inclusive global financial ecosystem.

Access to Global Investment Opportunities: Ensuring access to global investment opportunities is a key element of financial inclusion. Individuals, particularly in emerging economies, can benefit from investment diversification by participating in global financial markets. Facilitating access to investment instruments and providing education on investment strategies empower individuals to build wealth and secure their financial futures.

Challenges and Concerns in the Transition to Dedollarization

The transition to dedollarization, while holding the promise of a more diversified and resilient global financial system, is not without its challenges and concerns. One notable challenge lies in the potential for increased exchange rate volatility. As countries reduce their dependence on the US dollar, fluctuations in the values of alternative currencies may become more pronounced, introducing uncertainties for businesses, investors, and policymakers. Managing these currency risks becomes a critical aspect of the dedollarization process to ensure economic stability.

Another concern is the intricate task of reshaping existing financial infrastructures. The global financial system has long been anchored in the US dollar, and transitioning away from this established framework requires substantial adjustments. Adapting payment systems, financial regulations, and market practices to accommodate a more diverse set of currencies is a complex undertaking that demands careful coordination and international cooperation.

The impact on international trade is a central concern in the dedollarization transition. Given the historical dominance of the US dollar in trade transactions, recalibrating trade relations to accommodate a broader range of currencies raises questions about pricing mechanisms, trade agreements, and the overall efficiency of global commerce. Navigating these changes without disrupting established trade flows poses a significant challenge for nations aiming to dedollarise.

Furthermore, the potential for geopolitical tensions is a notable concern. The US dollar's role as the world's primary reserve currency has been closely tied to American influence in global affairs. As nations reduce their reliance on the dollar, shifts in economic power dynamics may lead to geopolitical frictions. Navigating these geopolitical challenges requires delicate diplomacy and strategic cooperation among nations undergoing dedollarization.

The risk of financial market disruptions is an additional concern during the dedollarization transition. Changes in currency preferences can impact the liquidity and stability of financial markets. Investors and financial institutions may face uncertainties regarding asset valuations, interest rates, and the overall functioning of markets. Implementing effective risk management strategies is crucial to mitigate the potential disruptions and ensure the stability of the global financial system.

Moreover, the socio-economic impact on individuals and businesses must be carefully considered. Currency transitions can affect purchasing power, savings, and the overall cost of living. Governments and financial institutions need to implement measures to protect vulnerable populations and ensure a smooth socio-economic transition during the dedollarization process.

Addressing these challenges requires a coordinated and adaptive approach from the international community. Collaborative efforts in developing regulatory frameworks, risk management strategies, and mechanisms for smoothing currency transitions are essential. Additionally, transparent communication and public awareness campaigns are crucial to mitigating uncertainties and fostering a supportive environment for the dedollarization transition. While the move towards dedollarization holds long-term benefits, proactively addressing these challenges is imperative to ensure a stable and successful transition to a more diversified global financial landscape.

Addressing Trade Imbalances and Exchange Rate Volatility

Addressing trade imbalances and managing exchange rate volatility is a complex task that involves a combination of economic policies, international cooperation, and strategic interventions. Here are key considerations for addressing these challenges:

Policy Coordination: Effective coordination of economic policies among trading partners is essential in addressing trade imbalances. Countries need to collaborate on fiscal, monetary, and exchange rate policies to ensure a balanced and sustainable global economic environment. Aligning policies helps prevent the emergence of persistent trade imbalances and mitigates the impact of exchange rate fluctuations.

Exchange Rate Management: Central banks play a crucial role in managing exchange rates to minimize volatility. Adopting flexible exchange rate regimes allows currencies to adjust to economic fundamentals. However, central banks may intervene in currency markets when excessive volatility threatens economic stability. Well-calibrated interventions can help prevent abrupt and disruptive currency movements.

Macroprudential Policies: Implementing macroprudential policies, such as capital controls and regulations on financial institutions, can contribute to stability in the face of exchange rate volatility. These policies help manage capital flows, reducing the risk of speculative activities that can exacerbate currency fluctuations and trade imbalances.

Trade Policy Adjustments: Countries may consider adjustments to trade policies to address imbalances. This could involve measures such as tariff modifications, trade agreements, and trade facilitation initiatives. By promoting a more equitable trade environment, nations aim to reduce trade imbalances and create conditions for sustainable economic growth.

Structural Reforms: Addressing trade imbalances often requires structural reforms to enhance economic competitiveness. This includes investing in education and workforce development, improving infrastructure, and fostering innovation. Structural reforms contribute to the diversification and upgrading of economies, making them more resilient to external shocks.

International Cooperation: Coordinated efforts on a global scale are crucial to addressing trade imbalances. Countries can engage in multilateral dialogues and negotiations to develop common frameworks for managing trade relations. International institutions, such as the International Monetary Fund (IMF), can facilitate discussions and provide guidance on policies that promote balanced trade and exchange rate stability.

Transparent Communication: Transparent communication from central banks and governments is essential to managing market expectations and reducing uncertainty. Clarity regarding monetary and fiscal policies, as well as the commitment to addressing imbalances, helps stabilize exchange rates and fosters confidence among investors, businesses, and consumers.

Surveillance Mechanisms: Establishing surveillance mechanisms to monitor trade imbalances and exchange rate movements is crucial. Regular assessments of global economic trends, conducted by international organizations and institutions, provide early warnings of potential imbalances and allow for timely policy adjustments.

Gradual Adjustments: Sudden and drastic adjustments in exchange rates or trade policies can be disruptive. Gradual and well-communicated adjustments allow economies to adapt without causing shocks to the global economic system. This approach minimizes the risk of unintended consequences and provides stakeholders with the necessary time to adjust.

Managing Debt and Financial Market Risks during Transition

Managing debt and financial market risks during a period of transition, such as dedollarization, demands a judicious and strategic approach to safeguard economic stability. One critical aspect involves a prudent debt management strategy. Governments must assess their debt portfolios, considering the currency composition and maturity profiles. A transition period presents challenges, and refinancing or restructuring debt in a manner that aligns with the changing monetary landscape is essential. Collaborating with international financial institutions can provide support and expertise in navigating debt-related challenges during the transition.

Financial market risks are heightened during times of economic transition. Central to managing these risks is the implementation of effective risk management practices by financial institutions. This includes rigorous stress testing of portfolios, assessing liquidity positions, and ensuring that risk mitigation strategies are in place. Regulators play a crucial role in overseeing financial market activities, enforcing prudential standards, and intervening when necessary to maintain market stability. Coordinated efforts between central banks and regulatory bodies are vital to address emerging financial market risks during the transition period.

Currency risk management is a pivotal consideration in a dedollarization transition. Businesses and financial institutions need to adapt to a more diverse currency environment, which involves careful evaluation of foreign exchange exposures. Utilizing financial instruments such as currency derivatives can help mitigate the impact of exchange rate fluctuations. Central banks, in collaboration with financial institutions, play a key role in providing guidance and ensuring that currency risk management practices are robust and aligned with the goals of the dedollarization process.

Transparency in financial reporting and communication is paramount during the transition period. Governments and financial institutions should provide clear information about their debt positions, risk management strategies, and the overall economic outlook. Transparent communication fosters trust in financial markets and allows stakeholders to make informed decisions, contributing to the stability of the financial system.

Collaboration with international partners is crucial in managing debt and financial market risks during a period of transition. Engaging in dialogue with international financial institutions, neighboring countries, and major trading partners can provide valuable insights and support. Coordinated efforts in risk assessment, policy formulation, and crisis management contribute to a more resilient global financial system.

Investor confidence is a linchpin in managing financial market risks. Governments and financial institutions must demonstrate a commitment to economic stability, sound fiscal policies, and effective risk management. Communicating clear and credible strategies for navigating the transition instills confidence in investors, reducing the likelihood of market disruptions.

Mitigating Potential Disruptions in the Global Financial System

Mitigating potential disruptions in the global financial system is a complex task that requires proactive measures, international cooperation, and a comprehensive understanding of potential risks. Here are key considerations for mitigating disruptions and fostering stability:

Risk Assessment and Scenario Analysis: Central to mitigating potential disruptions is a rigorous assessment of risks and scenario analysis. Governments, central banks, and financial institutions need to identify potential sources of disruption, evaluate their impact, and develop contingency plans. Scenario analysis helps in preparing for a range of potential outcomes and ensures a more resilient financial system.

International Cooperation and Coordination: Given the interconnected nature of the global financial system, international cooperation is paramount. Nations, central banks, and international organizations must collaborate to share information, coordinate policies, and address cross-border implications of potential disruptions. Collective efforts contribute to a more cohesive and synchronized response to challenges.

Effective Regulatory Oversight: Robust regulatory oversight is essential to maintain the integrity and stability of financial markets. Regulators play a crucial role in ensuring that financial institutions adhere to prudent risk management practices, have adequate capital buffers, and operate within a framework that safeguards the interests of investors and the overall stability of the financial system.

Stress Testing and Resilience Building: Conducting stress tests on financial institutions and the broader financial system helps assess their resilience to adverse conditions. Identifying vulnerabilities and weaknesses allows for preemptive measures to be taken to enhance the resilience of the financial system. Building resilience involves reinforcing risk management frameworks and ensuring that financial institutions have the capacity to withstand shocks.

Transparent Communication: Transparent communication from central banks, regulatory authorities, and governments is vital in mitigating disruptions. Clear and timely communication helps manage market expectations, reduces uncertainty, and fosters confidence among investors, businesses, and the public. Transparent communication is a key element in maintaining trust in the financial system.

Liquidity Support Mechanisms: Establishing liquidity support mechanisms is crucial in times of potential disruptions. Central banks can play a pivotal role in providing liquidity to financial institutions facing liquidity challenges. Well-designed liquidity facilities contribute to the stability of financial markets and prevent liquidity crises from escalating into more systemic issues.

Adaptive Monetary Policies: Central banks should adopt adaptive monetary policies that consider the evolving economic landscape. Flexibility in adjusting interest rates and unconventional monetary tools allows central banks to respond effectively to changing conditions. A forward-looking approach to monetary policy contributes to economic stability and mitigates potential disruptions.

Cybersecurity Measures: In the digital era, cybersecurity is a paramount concern. Potential disruptions can stem from cyber threats targeting financial institutions and critical infrastructure. Implementing robust cybersecurity measures, regular audits, and collaborative efforts to share threat intelligence contribute to protecting the financial system from cyber risks.

Social Safety Nets and Economic Support: Governments should have social safety nets and economic support mechanisms in place to mitigate the social impact of potential disruptions. Providing support to vulnerable populations during economic challenges helps maintain social cohesion and prevents the exacerbation of financial disruptions into broader societal issues.

Continuous Monitoring and Adaptation: Mitigating potential disruptions requires continuous monitoring of economic and financial indicators. Authorities should remain vigilant, adapting policies and measures as needed. A proactive and adaptive approach ensures that the financial system remains resilient in the face of evolving challenges.

The Future of Global Financial Systems without Dollar Dominance

The envisaged future of global financial systems without dollar dominance suggests a profound reconfiguration of the international monetary landscape. This shift is anticipated to usher in an era characterized by greater currency multipolarity, challenging the longstanding supremacy of the US dollar in global transactions. As nations increasingly diversify their foreign exchange reserves, alternative currencies such as the euro and the Chinese yuan are expected to play more prominent roles, leading to a rebalancing of economic power on the global stage.

One significant aspect of this future is the potential rise of regional currencies, as nations within economic blocs strengthen their monetary positions. This trend could foster increased intra-regional trade and economic cooperation, signaling a departure from the traditional reliance on a single global reserve currency. It might also give impetus to the development of localized financial ecosystems that cater to the specific needs of regional economic actors.

The evolution of payment systems is anticipated to be a pivotal feature in a world without dollar dominance. The advancement of digital currencies and blockchain technologies could reshape the mechanics of global payments. Central bank digital currencies (CBDCs) and decentralized finance (DeFi) platforms might become integral components of the financial infrastructure, offering efficiency, transparency, and accessibility in international transactions.

The anticipated diversification of reserve holdings is poised to bring about changes in the composition of countries' foreign exchange reserves. A departure from an overreliance on the US dollar could lead to increased holdings of alternative currencies, commodities, and other assets. This strategic diversification aims to reduce vulnerability to currency fluctuations and enhance the stability of nations' reserve portfolios.

The changing dynamics of global financial systems without dollar dominance are likely to influence the monetary policy decisions of central banks. Interest rates, inflation targeting, and other policy tools may undergo adjustments to align with the emerging global currency landscape. This could necessitate increased collaboration among central banks to maintain the stability of the international monetary system.

Beyond the economic sphere, the geopolitical ramifications of reduced dollar dominance are anticipated. Nations historically tied to the dollar may forge new economic alliances and strengthen ties with emerging powers or regional partners. Geopolitical relationships may experience realignments as economic influence becomes more dispersed across a range of currencies, challenging existing power dynamics.

The transition away from dollar dominance is not without its challenges. Countries and businesses may encounter difficulties adapting to new currency environments, and uncertainties in financial markets could pose risks. Addressing these challenges will require coordinated international efforts and adaptive strategies to ensure a smooth and stable transition.

In this evolving landscape, international organizations, particularly the International Monetary Fund (IMF), may assume a more substantial role. Reforms within these institutions may be necessary to accommodate the changing financial dynamics and promote global monetary stability.

Ultimately, the future of global financial systems without dollar dominance presents a vision of increased multipolarity, technological innovation, and adaptability. While challenges are inherent in such a transformative process, the potential benefits include a more resilient, inclusive, and equitable global financial system. The successful realization of this vision hinges on international collaboration, innovative solutions, and the ability of nations to navigate the complexities of a changing monetary paradigm.

Envisioning a Multipolar Monetary System

Envisioning a multipolar monetary system entails a paradigm shift in the global economic order, characterized by the diversification of dominant currencies and a departure from the historical dominance of a single reserve currency. This transformative vision holds several key implications for the international monetary landscape.

One of the central features of a multipolar monetary system is the emergence of multiple reserve currencies with increased prominence on the global stage. Beyond the traditional dominance of the US dollar, currencies such as the euro, Chinese yuan, and potentially others, could assume more significant roles. This diversification aims to distribute economic influence more broadly, reducing the vulnerability of the global financial system to shocks in any single currency.

Regional currencies are expected to play a pivotal role in the envisioned multipolar monetary system. Economic blocs and regional collaborations may strengthen their currencies, fostering increased intra-regional trade and financial cooperation. This regional emphasis could lead to the development of financial ecosystems that cater to the specific needs and dynamics of distinct geographic areas, promoting economic resilience and self-sufficiency.

The multipolar vision anticipates a redefinition of payment systems and financial transactions. Digital currencies and innovative technologies, such as blockchain and decentralized finance (DeFi), may gain prominence. Central bank digital currencies (CBDCs) could become integral components of the global monetary infrastructure, offering efficient and secure cross-border transactions. This technological evolution seeks to enhance the speed, transparency, and inclusivity of financial transactions on a global scale.

In a multipolar monetary system, the management of foreign

exchange reserves is expected to undergo a substantial transformation. Countries may adopt more diversified portfolios, reducing their dependence on a single reserve currency. This strategic diversification aims to mitigate risks associated with currency fluctuations and enhance the stability of national economies.

The envisioned multipolarity extends beyond economic considerations to geopolitical realignments. Nations may recalibrate their diplomatic and economic alliances, fostering greater cooperation with countries that hold prominent roles in the multipolar monetary system. This shift in geopolitical dynamics could lead to new patterns of collaboration and influence on the global stage.

A multipolar monetary system envisions a departure from the traditional reliance on a single economic powerhouse, promoting a more equitable distribution of economic influence. This transformative vision encourages nations to collaborate on an equal footing, fostering a sense of shared responsibility for global economic stability. The International Monetary Fund (IMF) and other international institutions may need to adapt to this multipolar reality, providing a platform for dialogue and cooperation among nations with diverse economic interests.

Potential Scenarios and Implications for Global Stability

Examining potential scenarios and implications for global stability involves contemplating a range of future developments that could shape the international landscape. These scenarios encompass economic, political, and social dimensions, each carrying unique consequences for global stability.

Economic Rebalancing: A scenario of successful economic rebalancing, where countries diversify their economic dependencies and reduce reliance on a single dominant currency, could contribute to increased stability. Such a shift may mitigate the impact of economic shocks and reduce vulnerabilities associated with the concentration of economic power, fostering a more resilient global economy.

Geopolitical Shifts: The emergence of new geopolitical alignments and power dynamics is another potential scenario. If nations successfully navigate a multipolar world, forging cooperative relationships and mitigating conflicts, global stability could be enhanced. Conversely, geopolitical tensions and realignments may pose challenges, impacting economic and political stability on an international scale.

Technology and Innovation: In a scenario where technological advancements and innovations drive economic growth and societal progress, global stability may benefit. Technologies such as artificial intelligence, renewable energy, and digital currencies could contribute to increased efficiency, resource sustainability, and inclusive economic development. However, the uneven distribution of technological benefits could exacerbate disparities and create new challenges.

Climate Change Mitigation: A successful scenario in mitigating climate change and promoting sustainable practices could contribute to global stability. International cooperation to address environmental challenges may foster resilience against climate-related disruptions, ensuring the stability of ecosystems, economies, and societies. Conversely, insufficient efforts to address climate change could lead to increased instability due to environmental and resource-related conflicts.

Inclusive Global Governance: A scenario where nations embrace inclusive and cooperative global governance structures may enhance stability. Strengthening international institutions, promoting multilateralism, and addressing global challenges collectively can foster a sense of shared responsibility. However, a lack of global cooperation or the rise of unilateral approaches could lead to increased geopolitical tensions and instability.

Social and Economic Inclusion: A future where social and economic inclusion is prioritized may contribute to global stability. Policies that address inequality, promote education, and ensure access to basic needs can enhance societal resilience and reduce the risk of social unrest. Conversely, persistent disparities in income and opportunities could lead to social and political instability.

Public Health Preparedness: The successful management of global health crises is a critical scenario for stability. Strengthening international cooperation on healthcare, pandemic preparedness, and vaccine distribution can mitigate the impact of health emergencies. Inadequate responses or the emergence of new health threats could pose challenges to global stability.

Technological Risks: A scenario involving technological risks, such as cyber threats or the misuse of emerging technologies, could undermine global stability. Insufficient cybersecurity measures, technological vulnerabilities, or the weaponization of advanced technologies may pose risks to economic and political systems.

Economic Downturn: An economic downturn scenario, triggered by financial crises, trade disruptions, or other factors, could pose challenges to global stability. Coordinated international responses, robust financial regulations, and effective crisis management mechanisms may be necessary to mitigate the impact and prevent prolonged economic instability.

Cooperation and Coordination Among Nations in a Dedollarized World

Cooperation and coordination among nations in a dedollarized world are paramount to ensure a smooth and stable transition, foster economic resilience, and mitigate potential challenges. In this transformed financial landscape, characterized by reduced dependence on the US dollar, collaborative efforts become essential for the well-being of the global economy.

Multilateral Dialogue and Agreements: Nations must engage in multilateral dialogues and agreements to establish common frameworks for economic cooperation and trade. Multilateral institutions, such as the International Monetary Fund (IMF) and the World Bank, can serve as platforms for fostering understanding and cooperation among nations undergoing dedollarization.

Currency Swap Agreements: Bilateral and multilateral currency swap agreements become instrumental in promoting financial stability. These agreements enable countries to trade and conduct financial transactions using their respective currencies, reducing dependence on a single reserve currency. Establishing and expanding such arrangements strengthen economic ties and provide liquidity support.

Harmonized Regulatory Standards: Harmonizing regulatory standards is crucial to ensure the stability and integrity of the global financial system. Common regulatory frameworks, transparent reporting standards, and collaborative oversight mechanisms help prevent regulatory arbitrage and create a level playing field for financial institutions across borders.

Transparent Communication: Transparent communication among nations is essential to build trust and manage expectations during the dedollarization process. Governments, central banks, and financial institutions should share information about their policies, strategies, and economic conditions. Transparent communication helps mitigate uncertainties, reduce market volatility, and enhance global economic stability.

Collaborative Monetary Policy Coordination: Central banks need to coordinate monetary policies to avoid disruptions in currency markets. This coordination ensures that adjustments to interest rates, inflation targeting, and other monetary tools are implemented in a way that promotes stability and prevents excessive volatility in exchange rates.

Joint Efforts in Financial Inclusion: Collaborative efforts in financial inclusion can address disparities in access to financial services. Nations can share best practices, technologies, and policies that promote inclusive financial systems, ensuring that the benefits of dedollarization reach a broader segment of the population.

Cooperative Climate Action: Nations can collaborate on climate action initiatives to address environmental challenges. Dedollarization provides an opportunity to integrate sustainable practices into economic policies, fostering cooperation in mitigating climate change and promoting green and resilient economies.

Shared Cybersecurity Initiatives: In a dedollarized world, nations must work together to enhance cybersecurity measures. The interconnectedness of financial systems requires collaborative efforts to prevent and respond to cyber threats. Information sharing, joint cybersecurity exercises, and the development of international cybersecurity standards are critical components of such cooperation.

Development of International Payment Systems: Collaboration in the development of international payment systems can facilitate efficient and secure cross-border transactions. Nations can work together to establish interoperable systems, adopt common standards, and promote the use of digital currencies, enhancing the efficiency of global payment networks.

Crisis Response Coordination: In times of economic challenges or crises, nations should coordinate their responses to prevent systemic disruptions. Collaborative crisis management strategies, such as coordinated fiscal stimulus and international support mechanisms, contribute to stabilizing economies and maintaining confidence in the global financial system.

The Bricks Alliance Role in Dedollarization

The BRICS alliance, comprising Brazil, Russia, India, China, and South Africa, assumes a pivotal role in the ongoing process of dedollarization, presenting a collective effort to reshape the international monetary landscape. As these emerging economies strive to diversify their financial interactions away from the dominance of the US dollar, the BRICS nations collectively contribute to fostering a more balanced and resilient global economic order.

At the forefront of the BRICS alliance's role in dedollarization is the promotion of currency cooperation and bilateral agreements. By encouraging the use of national currencies in trade and financial transactions among member nations, the alliance seeks to reduce reliance on the US dollar, fostering a more independent and diversified monetary environment.

The development of a common payment system emerges as another significant avenue for the BRICS alliance in its dedollarization endeavors. Through collaborative efforts, these nations can establish a seamless and secure payment infrastructure, diminishing dependence on external financial systems and paving the way for an alternative to the prevalent dollar-centric payment networks.

In parallel, the BRICS alliance can stimulate regional and bilateral trade agreements among its member nations. By endorsing the use of local currencies in trade settlements, the alliance aims to strengthen economic cooperation, diminish the influence of the US dollar, and promote a more decentralized and inclusive approach to international trade.

The coordination of monetary policies among BRICS central banks stands as a critical aspect of the alliance's role in dedollarization. Aligning policies contributes to the stability of member countries' currencies and enables a collective response to external economic challenges, fostering resilience in the face of global economic uncertainties.

The BRICS alliance can leverage regional financial institutions, particularly the New Development Bank (NDB) and the Contingent Reserve Arrangement (CRA), to provide alternative sources of financing. Strengthening these institutions contributes to economic stability among member nations and reduces reliance on dollar-dominated financial assistance.

Furthermore, the alliance can facilitate strategic collaboration in sectors such as infrastructure, energy, and technology. By pooling resources and coordinating investments, the BRICS nations can drive economic development within the alliance, diminishing the need for external financing predominantly denominated in US dollars.

In the realm of digital currencies, the BRICS alliance can explore and advocate for the adoption of digital currencies as viable alternatives. By collectively engaging in the development and implementation of digital currencies, these nations contribute to the diversification of the global financial system.

Advocating for reform in international financial institutions is also within the purview of the BRICS alliance's dedollarization strategy. By collectively pushing for changes in voting rights, representation, and the recognition of alternative reserve currencies, the alliance aims to better align these institutions with the evolving global economic landscape.

China & Russia roles in Dedollarization

China and Russia play crucial roles in the global dedollarization efforts, leveraging their economic influence, strategic partnerships, and policy initiatives to reduce dependence on the US dollar in international transactions. Their concerted efforts contribute to reshaping the international monetary landscape and fostering a more diversified and resilient global financial system.

China's Role:

China, as the world's second-largest economy, is at the forefront of dedollarization initiatives. The country has undertaken several strategic measures to promote the use of its currency, the yuan (renminbi), in international trade and finance.

- **Internationalization of the Yuan:** China has actively promoted the internationalization of the yuan by encouraging its use in trade settlements, investment, and as a reserve currency. The inclusion of the yuan in the International Monetary Fund's (IMF) Special Drawing Rights (SDR) basket in 2016 marked a significant milestone in this process.
- **Bilateral Currency Agreements:** China has entered into various bilateral currency swap agreements with several countries, allowing for trade to be conducted in local currencies rather than the US dollar. These agreements contribute to dedollarization efforts by reducing reliance on the dollar in bilateral transactions.
- **Digital Currency Initiatives:** China has been developing its central bank digital currency (CBDC), known as the digital yuan or e-CNY. The rollout of a digital currency offers an alternative to traditional currencies and enhances China's position in the global push for dedollarization.

Russia's Role:

Russia, with its vast natural resources and geopolitical influence, is actively pursuing dedollarization strategies to mitigate economic vulnerabilities and enhance financial sovereignty.

- **Diversification of Reserves:** Russia has been diversifying its foreign exchange reserves by reducing its holdings in US dollars and increasing its holdings in other currencies and assets. This move is aimed at minimizing exposure to the fluctuations of the US dollar and promoting a more balanced reserve portfolio.

- **Bilateral Trade Agreements:** Russia has entered into bilateral trade agreements with various nations to conduct transactions in national currencies, bypassing the US dollar. These agreements contribute to dedollarization efforts by creating alternative channels for international trade.
- **Gold Reserves Accumulation:** Russia has been accumulating gold reserves as a strategic move to reduce reliance on fiat currencies, including the US dollar. Gold is considered a hedge against currency fluctuations and provides a tangible asset in times of economic uncertainty.
- **Development of a National Payment System:** Russia has taken steps to develop a national payment system that reduces dependence on international payment systems dominated by the US dollar. This initiative enhances financial autonomy and contributes to dedollarization efforts.

Joint Efforts:

China and Russia, as strategic partners, have collaborated on various initiatives that align with dedollarization goals. The two nations have conducted bilateral trade in their respective currencies, bypassing the US dollar, and have explored joint ventures in the energy sector using non-dollar payment mechanisms.

The Way Forward: Embracing Dedollarization

The way forward involves a deliberate and strategic embrace of dedollarization, marking a paradigm shift in the global economic landscape. Nations around the world are recognizing the need to reduce dependence on the US dollar to enhance economic resilience, foster financial sovereignty, and promote a more equitable international monetary system.

As countries embark on this journey, one crucial aspect is the promotion of alternative reserve currencies. Diversifying foreign exchange reserves with a basket of currencies beyond the US dollar contributes to a more stable and balanced global financial system. This move not only mitigates the risks associated with the fluctuations of a single currency but also reflects a commitment to a multipolar economic order.

Simultaneously, the development and adoption of digital currencies emerge as a transformative element in dedollarization. Central bank digital currencies (CBDCs) and decentralized digital assets provide efficient, secure, and transparent means of conducting international transactions. Embracing these technological innovations contributes to the creation of a more inclusive and technologically advanced financial ecosystem.

Bilateral and multilateral agreements to conduct trade in local currencies play a pivotal role in reducing reliance on the US dollar. Such agreements foster economic cooperation and strengthen the financial independence of participating nations. As more countries engage in direct currency swaps and settlement mechanisms, the foundations for a dedollarized global economy are solidified.

Furthermore, fostering international collaboration among nations is essential. Joint initiatives, shared research efforts, and coordinated policy frameworks create an environment conducive to successful dedollarization. Multilateral forums and organizations become crucial platforms for dialogue, fostering understanding, and building consensus on the principles that underpin a more diverse and resilient global financial system.

A commitment to sustainable and inclusive economic practices is integral to the dedollarization journey. Nations can leverage this opportunity to integrate principles of environmental and social responsibility into their economic policies. Aligning dedollarization efforts with sustainable development goals ensures that the transition is not only economically sound but also socially and environmentally conscious.

In navigating the way forward, it is essential for nations to recognize the interconnectedness of their economies. A collaborative approach that transcends geopolitical differences and promotes shared economic objectives becomes imperative. dedollarization offers the prospect of a more cooperative and equitable international order, where nations collectively shape a financial system that is resilient, inclusive, and reflective of the diverse economic strengths across the globe.

References

Eichengreen, Barry. (2011). Exorbitant Privilege: The Rise and Fall of the Dollar and the Future of the International Monetary System.

- Eichengreen's work delves into the historical trajectory of the US dollar, providing insights into its ascent as a global reserve currency and contemplating its future role.

Prasad, Eswar S. (2014). The Dollar Trap: How the U.S. Dollar Tightened Its Grip on Global Finance.

- Prasad's examination of the intricate web of global finance highlights the challenges posed by the dominance of the US dollar and explores potential alternatives.

Rey, Hélène. (2015). Dilemma not Trilemma: The Global Financial Cycle and Monetary Policy Independence.

- Hélène Rey's research contributes valuable perspectives on the challenges faced by nations seeking to maintain monetary policy independence in the context of a global financial cycle dominated by the US dollar.

REFERENCES

Agarwal, Jamshed. (2020). The Death of the Dollar: A New World Money.

- Agarwal's exploration of the evolving role of the US dollar provides insights into the potential shifts in the global monetary landscape.

Ocampo, José Antonio. (2019). Resetting the International Monetary (Non)System.

- Ocampo's analysis offers a critical examination of the existing international monetary system and proposes potential reforms to address challenges associated with dollar dominance.

BIS (Bank for International Settlements) Annual Report.

- The BIS Annual Report provides a comprehensive overview of global monetary and financial trends, offering insights into the dynamics influencing the international monetary system.

International Monetary Fund (IMF) Publications.

- Various reports and working papers from the IMF offer rigorous analyses of global economic trends, currency dynamics, and policy implications, serving as valuable references for a comprehensive exploration of dedollarization.

Bowman, Robert G., and Swanson, Eric T. (2020). Assessing the Global Impact of the Dollar's Decline.

· This research paper offers an assessment of the potential global impact of a declining US dollar, shedding light on the implications for various economies.

Gourinchas, Pierre-Olivier, and Rey, Hélène. (2007). International Financial Adjustment.

www.ingramcontent.com/pod-product-compliance
Lightning Source LLC
Chambersburg PA
CBHW071536150726
48000CB00002B/825